TROLLING FOR STRIPED BASS AND BLUEFISH

TROLLING FOR STRIPED BASS AND BLUEFISH

Pete Barrett

BURFORD
BOOKS

Printed in the United States of America.

10   9   8   7   6   5   4   3   2   1

Library of Congress Cataloging-in-Publication Data
    Barrett, Pete.
    Trolling for striped bass / Pete Barrett.
        p.   cm.
    1. Striped bass fishing.   2. Trolling (Fishing).   I. Title.
SH691.S7B37   2006
799.17'732—dc22

                                    2006101944

DEDICATION

With special thanks to my wife, Linda, who supports my fishing obsession and shares time on the water with me. She is my life's partner and helped prepare this book every step of the way with suggestions, editing and encouragement.

And, to my son, Rich, who has traveled and fished far beyond the scope of my dreams and abilities. I cherish his inspiration and appreciate the time we share on the water; the student has become my teacher.

CONTENTS

Introduction

It's Vince Grippo's fault I caught the striped bass fever. I first met him in the 1960s working weekends pumping gas at a service station next to his hairdressing salon. I often fueled up his 'Vette, but conversations were little more than "Hi. How are you?"

That changed one morning when he pulled up to the pump with a big striped bass lying on a mat on the passenger seat. Vince had wrapped the bass in a towel, put a hat on it and intended to have a joke on my boss. For a kid who had only seen fish that big in the pages of *Outdoor Life*, this was an amazing catch. Forget the joke, I wanted to know where he caught the fish! I bombarded him with questions, which, like any good bass fisherman, he avoided answering; but he did agree to take me fishing with him.

I waited two years. We lived in the same town so occasionally we talked, and eventually he did take me fishing. We pushed off in his "tin" boat from the surf at Sea Bright, New Jersey, trolled wire line and caught several striped bass up to 15 pounds, and a few bluefish. I was wet and chilled to the bone, and unable to fight off the striped bass fever. That trip was the first of many experiences with Vince.

He made the symptoms worse by opening the door to his basement workshop where all kinds of strange tubes, bunker spoons,

Vince Grippo with a pair of striped bass caught on the troll in November of 1977.

wooden lures, rods and reels, and tackle hung from every inch of the rafters. I fished with Vince and his buddies more often, and learned to catch striped bass on live bunker, bucktails and plugs; but the days spent trolling with umbrella rigs and spoons from Monomoy, Massachusetts to central Jersey were the most enjoyable. Vince let me run the boat at times, patiently explained how to approach structure, how to interpret the graph recorder (remember them?), how to maneuver through the fleet, how to work the lines and how to get back in position on the trolling set to catch fish number two after number one was hooked up. It was an amazing chance to learn from a talented fisherman; an opportunity I didn't fully appreciate until years later after Vince passed away much too early.

In the following years, I was further blessed with days on the water with bass fanatics like Al Ristori, Al Reinfelder, Russ Wilson, Bob Orrok and Vic Galgano, and local charter skippers like Joe Renzo, Jim Donofrio, Mike Verges, Don Imbriaco, Bob Wallenstein, Joe Occhipinti and others. Just watching these guys run their boats, choreographing tackle and lures, was another education I could never duplicate. Each day was a grand adventure and a special thrill.

Since those amazing beginnings, I've been bitten by other fishing fevers, spent time chasing sharks, tuna and billfish in the bluewater, and traveled to some great fishing holes beyond my boyhood fantasies; but come spring and fall, I look forward to trolling for striped bass and bluefish. There's something magical about breaking the inlet at first light with the promise of a new day ahead and a chance to catch some of the greatest gamefish God ever put on the earth.

Catch 'em up!

TROLLING FOR STRIPED BASS AND BLUEFISH

CHAPTER 1

Challenges & Choices

There are many excellent reasons to troll for striped bass and bluefish, and like all fishing disciplines, trolling has its own unique challenges, choices and rewards. The most obvious challenge is the basic need to locate the fish; if you can't find the bass or blues, the best tackle, a secret lure and a tricked-out boat are worth absolutely nothing.

If you want to be more than "all show, and no go," the successful striped bass and bluefish troller must also become accomplished at boat handling, lure selection and tackle choices; and must be able to react to the sea, weather, tide changes, fish movements and nearby boat traffic. Trolling requires plenty of careful thought, a good memory and the ability to adjust and revise the day's fishing plan. There is no end to the education process, and every trip of each season adds to the collective encyclopedia of personal knowledge you will rely upon for future success.

The selection of the lures you use will include the challenges of choosing between plugs, spoons or tubes; and then there are choices of color, action, speed and depth of the lure presentation. On a broad basis, these options change as spring becomes summer, and as summer fades into fall; and it can change on an hourly basis as the local environment and fishing conditions change from dark to bright sky, sandy bottom to dark rocky bottom, cool water to warm water, and clear water to cloudy.

Tackle choices are usually made way in advance of the fishing trip. Typically the off-season winter months is the time when new rods and reels are purchased and rigged in preparation for the coming year, but there are many daily choices that take into account ever-changing fishing situations. The best inshore trollers are always analyzing the conditions at hand, then choosing the right tackle for the job. Basic tackle choices include wire line, lead core, super braid, mono or downriggers; and in any given fishing night or day, it's possible to choose from several tackle options. Mono or braid might get the nod in shallow water at dawn close to the beach just beyond the wash of the surf, wire or lead core could be a better choice in the early morning as the fish head to deeper structure and by late morning when the fish are deep it may be time to put the downriggers to work. Every trolling opportunity requires daily tackle adjustments, or a completely different set of tackle.

Successfully trolling for striped bass and bluefish requires continual decision making along with the processing of a wide array of conditions and events that influence the success of the day. Orchestrating and planning the fishing strategy, and reacting to the changing fishing situations so the right tackle can be employed and the optimum boat speed selected to pull the best lure over the exact spot where stripers lie in wait, is all part of the unique challenge of trolling.

Trolling is a proven technique to catch big, trophy-size striped bass.

Some fishermen never quite get it right. Although they may luck into sufficient numbers of fish to maintain their ongoing interest, and to keep the mental "fire" going so they are hungry enough to want to try again; they rarely score good catches consistently. The most successful sharpies have met these challenges head on, kept accurate logbooks and developed an intuitive knowledge about striped bass that allows them to catch fish consistently even on the bad days. They don't chase radio rainbows, that idle chatter on the VHF that makes some anglers crank up the engines and run from spot to spot, nor do they follow second- and third-hand fishing reports, or blindly follow other boats racing up and down the beach. Instead, they use skills learned over many seasons to think, react and anticipate with a trolling plan based on past experience.

Trolling is well known as a technique for catching large numbers of striped bass in the school- to medium-size range and bluefish of all sizes, and so it has a lot of appeal to fishermen looking to ice down a good catch for dinner, or to boast back at the dock about how many fish they caught. Fortunately, federal and state regulations limit the number of stripers we can catch so no one can "load the boat" like many of us did 30 to 40 years ago before we knew better.

Trolling is also a proven technique used by those who want to score with big striped bass, and each season many cow stripers are caught, and hopefully released, because these are the breeders and the future of our fishery, while on the troll. My three personal-best striped bass of 54, 49 and 48 pounds were caught on the troll. The 54 pounder was caught on an umbrella rig off Monomoy, Massachusetts with Vince Grippo at the helm, which made me just the "winder and grinder" angler. The two 40s, however, were taken off New Jersey, one off the Arches at the Shrewsbury Rocks, the other in the deep water off what locals call the Highlands Bridge. While the 54 was a nice fish, the two 40s stand out more in my mind because I was at the helm for both fish, and also reeled them in. A lot more satisfaction is derived from fish you fooled and hooked with your own brainpower and planning than from fish someone else fooled for you.

The learning process to be good at trolling for striped bass and bluefish never ends. Every season brings new experiences and challenges, and, therefore, new rewards. It never gets boring and there is no finish line.

WHY TROLL?

Bass and blues can be caught from the surf or a jetty, in back bays, inshore while drifting with live bait, anchored with live or dead bait, on light tackle and fly rods, by deep jigging and by casting surface poppers. With so many choices at hand, "Why troll?" is a valid question.

To an addicted striped bass troller, a better question is, "Why not?" Trolling allows a smart boater to cover lots of territory, moving from one good structure location to another until a good catch is made, either by catching fish one at a time at several locations, or by finding that mother lode hot spot that seems to hold a good-size pod of fish that can't resist the lures. The basic trolling precept is to cover as much bottom as possible to put the lures in front of as many striped bass as possible. By contrast, bait fishermen, especially those who must anchor to ply their craft, are limited to fishing only one, or a few, locations in a day's fishing. The troller has complete freedom to move from place to place until fish are found. Baitfishing can be very productive at times, but if the fish aren't nearby the spot selected, the bait fisherman will spend a lot of time daydreaming about what he hopes to catch, rather than actually catching fish. The troller, even when the fishing is slow, keeps his mind busy by plotting how to approach the next piece of structure, and the next, and the next until a rod gets bent over at the strike of a bass. Ahhh, sweet success!

Catching striped bass on the troll takes dedication and hard work with unique challenges and special rewards like this 48 pounder.

Trolling is especially productive in spring and fall when striped bass and bluefish are on their annual migratory runs along the coast. In New England the trolling action may continue all through the summer, but further south, it's more seasonal. These fish are moving and may not remain in any one area for long periods of time. It can often be a here-today, gone-tomorrow proposition as fish are found stacked up on structure on one day, only to move on the next day to another structure along their migratory travels. These places may only be a hundred yards apart triggered by tidal changes, or they can be miles away, triggered by the migration ritual as fish move to their summering grounds. The trolling bluefish and striped bass fisherman is better able to search out these changing hot spots because he can cover a lot of territory.

As we'll see in the coming chapters, the troller can control the depth of the lure presentation to match the exact feeding depth of the fish. By fishing with mono or braided line, wire or leaded core, or a downrigger, depths of only a few feet to nearly 100 feet can be effectively trolled.

THE TROLLING BOAT

Forty years ago I thought I was king of the hill with a brand-new 14-foot Starcraft aluminum boat. It was extremely versatile, and completely capable of being launched at a conventional ramp or launched in the surf to get to good striper fishing. I fished it from Connecticut's Norwalk Islands, to Shelter Island in New York, in the Hudson River's Croton Bay, in my home waters of New Jersey, and in the Delaware and Chesapeake Bays.

Surf launches were always an adventure. After a successful push-off, always in the back of your mind through the rest of the day was the thought that you had to navigate the surf again to beach the boat and get back to dry land. Launching and retrieving a "tin" boat from the beach was exciting, albeit hard work and the element of disaster with an overturned boat was always lurking. Along the Jersey Coast where I launched, a calming west wind was prayed for, and you never launched into a big easterly swell.

Small boats can also be launched any place where you can get access to water, not necessarily at a bonafide ramp. The end of a road with a gravel patch can be okay, or at worst, you can carry the boat to get into the water. It all depends on how hungry you are to catch the next bass or blue. There are many "casual" ramps all along the coast that cannot handle a big rig, but which are okay for a 12- to 16-foot aluminum boat, and for this reason, the small boats are a terrific option. Many a bass fanatic having graduated into a big boat still keeps a small skiff alongside the house "just in case."

Center console boats are in great favor because of their 360 degrees of fishing room, and boats of 17 to 25 feet are the most popular size. Recently, a new breed of 26- to 35-foot center console boats are also becoming very popular, rigged with two or three powerful outboard engines to attain great speed, and with a big fuel tank to increase the range of the boat. These deep-vee hulls cut through bad seas so anglers can travel great distances at speeds up to 40 or more knots to reach striped bass, and are especially popular with tournament anglers.

Spring and fall can be quite cold so many striped bass trollers prefer a boat with a small cuddy cabin. Tackle storage is dramatically improved, a head is usually included, plus a hard top with additional rod holders along its back edge, and a full canvas and isinglass enclosure to keep wind and rain out of the boat. The comfort level in a cuddy cabin boat is a big plus. There is something to be said for staying dry on a windy, 40 degree, late October day, when salt spray is drenching fellow anglers in their center console boats.

Larger boats with a full salon, or cabin, are also excellent choices, but they require a crew to operate, making one-man operation difficult. These floating condos are the ultimate in comfort and tackle storage, and also have the added benefit of handling sea conditions better. A heavy boat will plow through waves and chop providing a steady trolling speed, whereas smaller, lighter boats are more dramatically affected by waves and sea conditions. Big swells can momentarily stop a small boat when trolling against a sea, and then the boat speeds up as it goes down the back of the swell, only to slow down as the next swell builds up under the hull. A larger boat has a greater ability to plunge through bad seas.

Inboard engines are also a help when dealing with rough seas. A 30- to 40-foot diesel-powered boat can plow through choppy seas with relative ease, but outboards, and the lighter boats they get hung on, do not have the same momentum. It's like comparing horses (diesels) to ponies (outboards), and the horses simply have more push. Diesel boats often can troll slower than an outboard boat, which can sometimes be critically important.

Your pocketbook and budget, plus personal preferences, and the opinions and needs of your family will dictate the size, type and cost of the boat you purchase. There is no perfect striped bass boat and many addicted striped bass trollers will change boats several times in their lifetime, always with an eye toward fishing from a "better" boat.

Big or small, inboard or outboard, trolling boats with large cockpits and plenty of deck space make trolling a lot easier.

My own experiences began with a 14-foot aluminum skiff, but like many fishermen boaters, I had to have something bigger, and bigger, and bigger still. Over the past 40 years I've made the transition from aluminum skiff, to a 19- and then a 25-foot Mako center console, then to 32- to 39-foot diesel inboard express boats built by Topaz and Ricky Scarborough, restored a 31 Bertram Bahia Mar, and now run a 21-foot Parker center console. I'm back where I started!

Besides running my own boats for charter and personal fishing, I've also been blessed with the opportunity to fish with many other charter skippers along much of the East Coast and could pick up boat-handling tips and tricks that worked on my own boats. Many of the features that make a good trolling boat are just as important in Maine as they are at Montauk or at the Chesapeake Bay-Bridge Tunnel, so let's review the most important considerations.

Of primary importance is the size of the cockpit and how fishable it is. The cockpit can be defined as the area aft of the helm on express, cuddy and center console boats, or aft of the salon in a large convertible boat. The space needs to be large enough to allow two or more anglers to move around without being crowded. Boats with a long cockpit, measured from front to back, make a better bass boat than boats with a wide, but short cockpit. Down East and Chesapeake Bay boats usually have long cockpits and are much in demand by serious striper fishermen. Center console anglers can take advantage of the space alongside the console to add an extra measure of walk-around deck space and crew-friendly fishing room.

A deck that is wider than the top of the cover boards allows improved toe room and therefore more comfort and safety when standing at the gunnel, while setting out tackle and reeling in fish. Avoid padded gunnels, they reduce the cockpit size and hooks have a penchant for sticking into, and ruining, the vinyl covers.

The cockpit area has to be trolling-friendly with rod holders placed so that the skipper and crew can get at them without getting in each other's way. A free flow of the work (deck) space is important. Rod holders must be positioned about midway along the cover boards so the angler or mate responsible for letting out the line and then placing the rod in the trolling position can do so without having to struggle. Rod holders in the extreme corners of the stern are awkward and should be avoided. There should be sufficient space in the cockpit to store a gaff, large striper net, extra lures, back-up rods and reels pre-rigged and ready to fish.

The deck surface must have a non-skid pattern. A breezy day with a rockin' and rollin' boat can put a lot of water on the deck making it slippery and tough to walk on if you don't have your sea legs. Gunnel height should come to just above the knee for safety and for comfort while leaning against it to work the tackle and reel in fish. A gunnel that is too low is not safe, and too high makes it

The best trolling skiffs have wide open, uncluttered cockpits so the crew has plenty of working room.

difficult to work the tackle, to net or gaff the catch, and to release those fish you want to return to the fishery.

A fight chair is not needed, but a rocket launcher can be a valuable option to hold rods while traveling; and on cuddy or center consoles, the rocket launcher can also have a valuable storage box that holds terminal tackle, pliers, gloves, and extra gear.

Single engines are usually more economical, but twin engines add an extra measure of safety and maneuverability. Twin engine boats often troll too fast with both engines in gear, even at idle, so one engine will have to be shut down while trolling to achieve the correct lure speed. We'll cover more about this in the chapter on Trolling Strategies.

FISHING WITH A CHARTPLOTTER

A wide range of electronics is available to help you catch more striped bass on the troll, including safety items such as a VHF radio and radar; and in case you have a severe emergency and have to ditch, an EPIRB is good to have.

A chartplotter/fishfinder combination will add another important measure of safety as a navigation aid, but from a fish-finding point of view, the chartplotter/fishfinder is the most essential component of any electronics package; large boat or small, bay or offshore. The saltwater environment is not a friendly place for electronics and years ago fishfinders and positioning equipment, such as loran and early GPS models, sometimes failed. When manufacturers began combining the two into one dual-purpose unit, some fishermen worried that if it crashed, they would be left flying blind with no fishfinder and no way to locate their position, two vital pieces of information for successful fishing and catching of striped bass. The worries have proven baseless and failure of these units, though not impossible, has been extremely rare due to improved construction techniques.

Based on the satellite Global Positioning System (GPS) the chartplotter half of the combination displays an electronic navigational chart for the local area being fished, along with all the bottom

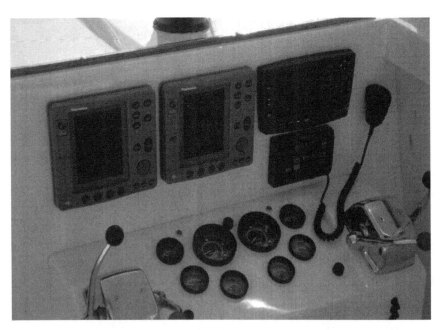

Essential trolling electronics include a colorscope, combination GPS and chartplotter, VHF radio and temperature gauge. For added safety, radar rounds out the package on this bass boat.

structure that hold striped bass and bluefish. A GPS can pinpoint the boat's position, and the location of bottom structure to within a scant few yards. Although some chartplotters are sold without a built-in fishfinder, striped bass trollers are better served with a built-in fishfinder that displays a perpetual updating of the bottom contours, fish marks and bait.

The Save, or Man Overboard (MOB), key is particularly useful because the strike location of every gamefish can be retained in the chartplotter memory chip with the simple press of the Save or MOB button. A chartplotter will not only display a chart of where you are located, along with bottom contours and channel markers, but it also plots, or tracks, the boat's progress on the screen with a dotted line as it travels from place to place. It will show you where you've been trolling, where the fish have been hitting (if you hit the Save or MOB button) and the route you traveled to and from the inlet and your home dock or launch ramp.

ROD AND REEL CHOICES

A wide variety of tackle can be employed to troll for striped bass, including spinning, light and heavy-duty conventional, and lever-drag reels. Which you use is dependent upon where and how you fish, and the size of the fish. Schoolie bass can be handled quite nicely on spinning gear trolled in a shallow bay, or in deep water on a downrigger. Medium and jumbo stripers call for heavier gear, of course, but with the increasing popularity of super-braid lines, traditional large conventional reels are being replaced with smaller, lighter graphite body or machined-aluminum reels that are quite capable of standing up to big fish.

Rod design and special needs dictate the choice of rods. Those anglers using super-braid lines are trending toward rods with a softer action to compensate for the lack of stretch of the braid. Bunker spoon specialists like soft, long rods to enhance the spoon's pulsating action and to help the lures swim better in rough water. An umbrella rig armed with a full compliment of soft-plastic shad bodies has an enormous amount of water resistance and needs a powerful rod. Trolling a back bay with sandworms is more productive with a conventional rod, but trolling wire line requires an entirely different approach.

Tackle choices are also dictated by the type of line used for trolling, such as monofilament, braid or wire, and specific tackle recommendations will be provided in the following chapters; but it is essential here to measure your commitment to trolling. You'll definitely be more successful with tackle dedicated specifically to trolling for stripers and blues. It's also important to fish your tackle in matched pairs so that the rod and reel outfits on both sides of the boat are identical. This will help you manage the trolling depths of the tackle, and make it much easier (as in tangle-free) to maneuver. Mismatching a wire-line outfit on one side and a mono outfit on the other is an invitation to a huge tangle, lots of frustration and possible loss of expensive lures and fishing time. Don't be a googan; invest in good tackle, fish it in pairs and reap the rewards of good catches of fish and enjoyable days on the water. Quality tackle can seem expensive at the outset, but since it lasts longer and helps you achieve a higher level of success, it is less expensive in the long view.

Big boats have plenty of storage space for extra gear and extra rods and reels. Fishing from a small boat, however, requires careful tackle selection, and choosing multi-purpose rods and reels is a big advantage. One such rod is the Lamiglas BL7030W. It is a superb choice for striper and bluefish trolling. Equipped with Fuji Silicon Nitride II guides, it can be used for wire, super braid, or mono, or fished with downriggers. The guides are tough enough to laugh at the abrasiveness of wire, and smooth enough to handle mono and super braids with a soft touch. If you prefer to build your own rods, the Silicon Nitride II guides are the ultimate choice.

Carrying spare reels allows the small-boat angler to switch from wire to super braid in just a few seconds without the need to invest in another pair of rods. Start the day with a pair of reels filled with 100 yards of wire line and keep a second pair of reels filled with 30 or 50-pound super braid or monofilament in your tackle bag. When you want to switch to super-braid techniques, or need mono for a downrigger, just switch the reels.

ACCESSORIES AND EQUIPMENT

Trolling for striped bass and bluefish requires only a few unique items to make fishing easier and more productive. Most fishermen already have the obvious fishing gear on board such as hook-outs, pliers, hand scales, sunglasses, foul weather gear and so forth, so let's not spend time discussing the obvious.

We all dream about that huge striped bass, a fish so big we won't have to exaggerate to our buddies (well, maybe just a little), and so we need to be prepared for that catch of a lifetime, even if most of the fish we score are not jumbo fish. Trolling puts a lot of stress on fishing tackle so safety equipment that keeps the tackle in the boat is essential. And, we need something to help maneuver the boat in tight quarters when there are many boats in a small area or when fishing tight areas.

OUTRODDERS are a handy way to achieve better line control and more maneuverability. Outrodders are T-shaped aluminum rod holders designed specifically for trolling with wire line, but they also work well with mono, lead core and super braids. They slip into a standard flush-mount rod holder positioned on top of the cover boards and hold the rod virtually parallel to the water and at 90 degrees from the boat. When trolling with wire line it is important to accurately calculate the trolling depth by measuring the wire line that is streaming in the water. The low profile of the outrodder keeps the line low to the water so more of it is actually in the water.

By keeping the rods at 90 degrees to the boat, the distance between the port and starboard trolling lines is not calculated based

Outrodder rod holders are mandatory for wire line trolling, because they keep rods low to the water and at 90 degrees to the side of the boat for maximum lure spread.

just on the width of the boat (about 8 to 12 feet); it's actually the width of the boat plus the bent length of the two rods (about 20 to 24 feet total), which allows dramatically improved maneuvering capabilities. Turns can be executed with less worry about lines tangling, a big concern when trolling wire line.

For small boats, a modified outrodder with an L-shape keeps the rod and reel closer to the angler and makes it a lot more convenient to remove the rod from the outrodder without having to lean over so far.

SAFETY LINES keep your tackle attached to the boat. Hang a big fish and there will be an enormous amount of pressure on the tackle, and the angler often has a tough time pulling the rod and reel from the outrider. Wet and slippery hands, a big fish and a rocking boat can all conspire in the worst way causing the angler to lose his grip on the tackle. I can tell you first-hand that losing a rod and reel overboard is not a happy experience; have this happen to you once and you'll become a safety-line fanatic. The loss of a mid-priced complete wire-line outfit can be in excess of $200 to $300—ouch!

Safety lines are easily made from ¼-inch, three-strand nylon line, cut to a length convenient for your boat's cockpit, which is usually around 6 to 12 feet. The simplest line has an eye spice at each end, one end is looped around the reel seat, and the other end is tied to the bottom of the flush-mount rod holder. There are some variations you may want to try, such as tying the safety lines to the base of a rocket launcher. If the reels have harness lugs on them, a stainless steel spring clip can be attached to one end of the safety line and clipped to the reel.

I also recommend a safety line for the outrodders. The above-mentioned loss of the rod and reel included the outrodder, which added to the financial pain. I recommend modifying the outrodder by replacing the gimbal pin with a stainless bolt having an eye at one end. They are readily available at most boating and marine supply stores. Run a short safety line from this eye bolt to the bottom of the flush-mount rod holder to hold the outrodder in place. The eye bolt can also be used as the attachment point for the rod and reel safety line.

A BIG NET is essential to comply with the size and bag limits of today's fishing world. Few anglers use a gaff these days, although it's still the best way to boat a big striper meant for the dinner table.

Daily bag limits vary from one or two stripers per day, depending on state fish and game regulations, which demands that we release most of the fish we catch. Those who remember the striped bass stock collapse of the 1980s are more than happy to comply, especially to release the big breeders for the continued good health of the striped bass stocks.

Because so many bass must be released, net selection is important to the survival of every striper returned to the water. Avoid nets with uncoated nylon or cotton webbing, and instead look for a net with the net bag coated with rubberized or a soft-plastic coating, such as the big nets marketed by Frabill. These coatings nearly eliminate the removal of the fish's protective slime coating so they are released in the best possible condition.

The size of the net bag depends upon the size of the fish being targeted. Back-bay schoolies don't require a huge net, but a back-bay net will self-destruct when it meets a 30-pound bass. I have two nets, and use the one that fits the day's fishing. Nets with a collapsible handle are handy because they stow away in minimal space.

GAFF CHOICES are not as important today as they were 40 years ago when anglers referred to their fish by weight, not inches. A "28" meant a 28-pound bass, not a 28-inch keeper. Because of size and daily bag limits most striped bass are released, making gaffs somewhat irrelevant. I still keep a gaff on board in case we meet that fabled 60 pounder, a fish so big that no net will be able to handle it. I might elect to release that trophy, but having a gaff on board leaves my options open. Some states limit the use of or the size of gaffs so check with your state fish and game department.

A good bass gaff has a 6-foot handle and a stainless steel hook with a 3-inch bite. Wrap the handle with cork rod-grip tape so you have more area to hold onto, and to provide a better griping surface.

LURE STORAGE deserves special mention because many of the popular striped bass trolling lures are very large in size and are too bulky to store conveniently. A bunker spoon doesn't fit a standard tackle box, nor does an umbrella rig, or a 24-inch eel tube. Striped bass fishermen have developed unique ways to store their gear and lures.

Bunker spoons can be stored in plastic shoe storage boxes, umbrella rigs can be folded to fit into a 1-gallon soda bottle with the top cut off, or stacked into a 5-gallon bucket. Tackle shops sell 3-inch diameter plastic tubes with slip-on end caps to hold umbrella and shad rigs. Many deep-diving plugs have swim lips that are too large to fit conventional lure storage trays, so inventive anglers use 9-inch lengths cut from clear plastic tubes used to protect fluorescent lights. Push a Snapple iced tea bottle cap into the bottom of the tube and you have a handy plug storage tube that can then be placed as a group into a 5-gallon bucket.

There's never enough tackle storage on small boats, so keeping your gear organized and dry is a challenge. Besides storing umbrella rigs, 5-gallon buckets with notches cut in the rim can provide handy storage for spoons, tubes, shads, deep-diving plugs, trolling eels, bucktails and parachute jigs.

A zippered canvas bag, like the ubiquitous L.L. Bean bag, is also a good choice to keep gear organized. It will hold gimbal belts and foul weather gear, jackets, sunglasses, and several Plano or Flambeau plastic boxes that will hold additional lures, rigs and tools.

GIMBAL BELTS provide a big measure of comfort when reeling in striped bass, especially if the bass are jumbo size and pull quite hard; and when using wire line and shad rigs where water resistance on the lures can make reeling in even without a fish to simply check the lures for weed an uncomfortable proposition. Small belts are just fine for striper trolling, so you don't need a big belt like the tuna boys use. Braid, Tsunami and others sell compact gimbal belts that offer plenty of protection so the rod butt won't dig into your gut and they are just fine for bass trolling. The best have a quick-snap release on the belt for fast and easy mounting of the belt.

CUSTOMIZED CHARTS

Although we rely on the electronic chart in the GPS chartplotter while we're on the water and running the boat, a printed chart showing the inshore structure is a handy pre-trip tool to help visualize where and how to troll while planning the next trip. A quick review of the chart the night before a trip is a good way to refresh your memory bank. It is also helpful when fishing new areas, to become more familiar with the local bottom structure.

NOAA charts show bottom structure in pale gray lines, which can be tough to see. Trace over them with a fine-line, permanent-ink marker and the structure will literally leap off the chart. Every lump, point, slough, ridge and potential bottom structure will be clearly identified. Charts can be stored in large Ziploc-style pouches sold in marine supply stores.

THE LITTLE BLACK BOOK

Like advice from a good real-estate agent, trollers must pay attention to location, location, location. For fishermen, it's spelled structure, structure, structure. The changing bottom contours provide the highways for game fish to move from one feeding station to another, and for baitfish to huddle in tight packs of false safety. Find the structure and you'll find the fish.

Fishfinders and colorscopes become the angler's eyes to peer below the surface to "see" the lumps, bumps, humps and drop-offs where striped bass and bluefish will lie in ambush for a quick, easy meal. Get a fishfinder with the largest screen that will fit on your boat. This is the "TV show" you'll watch all day as you search for bait and game fish.

As good as they are, the fishfinder and the chartplotter will only show what is available at any given moment today; and a collection of Saved locations where fish strikes occurred on previous trips. Neither of them can recall detailed history from years past, and without history, you can't predict the future. Knowing where the fish were located ten years ago, last year, and last week, can make today far more successful. Also of great value is the compilation of notes from the logbook about time, tide, weather, trolling direction and speed, lure type and color, trolling depth, tackle, moon phase and more. History is easy to record in your little black book, a small spiral notebook kept at the helm on every single trolling trip.

After several years of collecting numbers and locations, the best bass trollers develop an accurate profile and can predict where bass and blues will be found. Instead of trolling aimlessly, they focus on those specific locations where fish were caught in the past, and concentrate their efforts on these proven places.

Areas of fairly large bottom structure may not hold striped bass on every square foot of that bottom contour. Oftentimes the bass will hold in small, specific locations, and the savvy troller will present the lures to these small areas rather than waste precious trolling time where there are no fish. Like Rodney Dangerfield, the logbook gets "no respect" from many fishermen, but if you want to become more than a wannabe, a logbook is essential.

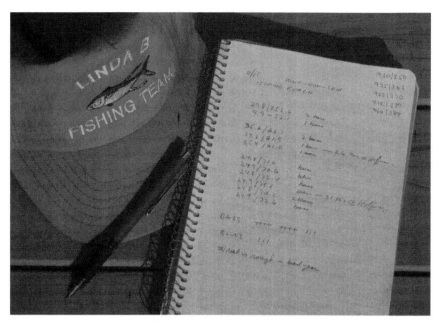

A detailed logbook will help you find more striped bass and bluefish on every fishing trip and they become more valuable as a reference as they accumulate more information.

Like the old saying, "Of all the things I've lost, I miss my mind the most," keeping an accurate up-to-date logbook will forever record all the important information that is needed to become a sharpie. Write it down and you can't forget! There is a consistency in striped bass fishing that is enhanced by keeping a logbook. The very act of writing down or logging in the day's events keeps our mind thinking and analyzing. Striped bass and bluefish return to the same locations with great predictability year after year. Knowing where, when and what you used to catch a fish this year, will be extremely valuable next year. Given similar fishable weather conditions, on or about the same date you'll probably find striped bass in the same location, on the same tide, ready to take the same lure.

GETTING COMFY

Spring and summer are pleasant times to fish, but late fall can be gruesome. The warm-weather seasons can dish out some rain and wind, which are easily overcome with good foul weather gear; but in late fall we also have to overcome extreme cold. Fair-weather fishermen will stay home when the weather is uncomfortable and risk the chance of missing some of the best bites of the year. The fish are already wet, and they don't care whether you are comfortable or not. Choppy seas, cloudy skies, maybe a rain shower and a brisk wind, all add up to ideal bass trolling conditions. To withstand these awful conditions, you need to dress the part.

After running his center console for 16 miles at 25 knots against a 15-knot north wind, a friend of mine once said, "I wish I had a face like a steel chisel to cut through this wind." With air temperatures near freezing, a breezy wind and a fast boat, it's easy to get windburn on your face and lips. The AquaSkinz dry hood, a 3mm neoprene pullover hood leaves only a small opening for nose and eyes and eliminates a lot of wind problems. Add a pair of clear safety goggles, or snowmobile goggles, and you'll protect your face and eyes from windburn. The Simms ExStream hat is an alternative choice with full head, neck and ear coverage. Also good is the simple wool Navy watch cap.

Late fall trollers don't need to make fashion statements, so the clothing they choose is for comfort only. Layering your clothing is the key to staying warm. Fishing from a cabin boat is certainly more comfortable, you can even turn a heater on to help chase away the cold; but cabin boat or center console, when it's bitter cold, you need to stay dry and warm. It's especially important in a center console because you are exposed to the raw elements for hours at a time.

Standard foul weather gear will do an adequate job if wind and spray is not overpowering. On those really bad days, however, when it's breezy and salt spray is flying everywhere, a waterproof top like the AquaSkinz Hurricane or hooded Rampage, worn over foul-weather bib pants are essential. Other good tops are made by Guy Cotton, Grundens and Helly Hansen, some have Polar fleece for warmth and poly sleeves and chest for waterproofing. Add a pair of AquaSkinz or Glacier gloves and you'll be dry and warm on most days.

Underneath the top, I like a light weight Polartec T-shirt, then a chamois or flannel shirt over that. I keep a jacket stowed away for midday when the air temps become more comfortable. If seas are calm, I can stow the neoprene top in favor of the mid-weight jacket.

Trolling is fun for young and old, and instills values of dedication, self-sacrifice, perseverance and commitment into a world full of video games and instant gratification.

Wet feet will ruin your day for sure. Heavy wool socks work well inside most any deck boot on the wettest days. When I expect calm seas and little spray, I like the traditional fleece-lined L.L. Bean zip-up boots for good traction and toasty toes.

Other good choices to stay warm are the Carhart jumpsuits, but the Mustang series of survival suits are the ultimate. They also offer the added safety advantage of floatation in the unlikely situation that you have to "jump ship" in extreme cold weather. Mustang manufactures a complete line of insulated, floatable bib pants, vests, coats and bomber-style jackets that are terrific for cold-weather fishing.

DEDICATION—COMMITMENT

The best trollers, sometimes called sharpies or pros in newspaper columns, reached their levels of success with dedication and commitment. Tackle, lures, equipment and the boat are only tools that help the best anglers use their brains, intuition and skills to make good catches happen for them.

Dedication means fishing when the tides are right for the fish, not you; at night, dawn and dusk; and at times when the weather is lousy and less committed anglers are home watching TV shows. Commitment means equipping yourself with quality tackle, and not cutting corners. It means taking time to keep a logbook, doing the pre-trip research, developing a network of fellow fishermen and tackle shops to share info, and to always being in tune with tide and moon phases. To do these things takes effort, and the willingness to take this extra effort is always a trait of the best fishermen.

A friend once joked that he got married "until striped bass do us part," and while I know plenty of good striped bass and blue fishermen that lead good family lives, it does illustrate the point that to be good, to be successful, you must be ready to fish when the conditions are right for the bass, not for you. You will have to lose some sleep, take a sick day here and there and physically inconvenience yourself at the peak striped bass season; but the rewards are well worth it.

Don't neglect your kids. In today's world of instant gratification, stupid TV shows and mind-numbing video games, the qualities of self-sacrifice, dedication and commitment have never been more important to pass along to your children. It is essential for them to learn that what they will earn in life depends upon what they spend. Without spending the effort to be dedicated and committed, they will earn or achieve little in return. Fishing offers dads and moms some wonderful opportunities to pass along meaningful experiences to their kids. Take the young ones fishing; they are tomorrow's future.

CHAPTER 2

Trolling Lures That Catch

Choosing a trolling lure is the defining moment at the start of each day's fishing. The color, size, action and silhouette are all-important considerations that often spell the difference between success and failure. Subconsciously we wonder if yesterday's hot lure will again be the winner today, or will it be a dud; and we wonder if we should try something different today that will be the hot new lure. The final decision is based upon our personal on-the-water experiences, tempered by recent fishing reports heard at tackle shops or on the docks from fellow striped bass and bluefish anglers.

The selection process includes many variables. We have to consider the trolling depth, the species of prevalent bait, time of day, ambient light and even the time of year. All these questions are critical to success. A lure that rides too high or too deep in the water column, or fails to match the local bait in shape and size, and which is too bright or too dark to be seen by stripers or blues will not catch many fish.

The most effective lure size, shape, color and action will often change with the seasons; the hot lures of spring when bluefish are near the surface as they invade coastal waters are not necessarily the best choice for fall when fish are schooled in tight packs down deep preparing to stage their reverse migration run to southern climes. The big-bass bunker spoons that imitate the jumbo-size menhaden of spring usually get put away in late June, and are replaced by shad rigs, which imitate the massive schools of smaller peanut bunker and mullet.

Making these decisions and solving these "fishy" problems, is what makes trolling so interesting. The angler who snaps on any old lure with little thought about what will work best is doomed to minimal success.

COLOR

Water clarity, depth and ambient light have a dramatic influence on the effectiveness of any lure. In cloudy water, a lure's ability to reflect its color is dramatically minimized, and as a fish's ability to see becomes restricted, it relies more on its ability to pick up vibrations through the lateral line. When encountering cloudy water conditions, bright lures, such as white, lime green, pink or yellow may trigger a strike simply because the color is so much more visible than muted colors such as black, dark red, purple and clear. Although these bright attractor colors imitate nothing found naturally in the ocean, striped bass and bluefish may strike simply because they can see the lure.

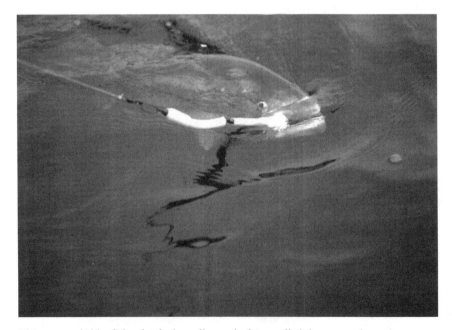

This mean ol' bluefish whacked a yellow tube lure pulled deep on a downrigger using light tackle.

Light is made up of many wavelengths, and a lure's color is dependent upon how well it reflects that color's wavelength back to the eye of the beholder; fish or man. Green is green because it does not reflect red, blue and yellow. The green is bounced back to the eye; the other colors are absorbed into the lure.

Because not all wavelengths penetrate water equally and since the color of a lure is based upon light waves bouncing off its surface, for a color to exist in water, light waves must be able to penetrate below the surface. Some wavelengths do not penetrate very deeply into the water, and that's why red virtually disappears as a color only a few feet below the surface. Its light waves penetrate only a few feet, while lime green, with light waves that deeply pierce the water, retains a lot more of its color in clear water even 30 feet below the surface.

When choosing lure colors, we also have to consider that in the fish's watery world, few colors look the same as they do in the air. The greenish-blue tint of the water alters the underwater perception of every color. The white bunker spoon, plastic shad or wooden trolling plug takes on a pale blue-green tint because of the

A red tube fooled this striped bass, but tomorrow the hot lure may be a plug spoon or bucktail. The troller is always ready to meet the challenges of every fishing day.

natural hue of the water. Yellow picks up the blue-green tint and becomes slightly greener beneath the water's surface. Dark colors are less influenced by the ambient tint of the water.

Some colors imitate natural bait; others serve as attractors only and have no seeming relationship to anything that swims in the ocean. Chartreuse is a favorite color, so is pink, yet no one has ever seen a chartreuse baitfish, squid or sea worm. Bright colors trigger an attack response because they are highly visible, a situation which is common in summer when plankton bloom by the billions and make the water murky, or when rain waters wash mud from nearby rivers. The bright chartreuse, pink, yellow or white lure can be seen, so it gets the strikes.

Any discussion of lure color should also include a factor I call "flash." Lures with a shiny silver or gold-chromed finish, polished stainless steel spoons and swimming plugs with sparkles in the finish all reflect a bright flash as the lures swim, pulsate and wobble while being towed at the end of the trolling line. Even if the fish does not see the lure's color very well, it will probably see and react to the lure's flash. A bright, flashy lure is, therefore, often the best choice.

LURE ACTION

Wouldn't it be great if we could talk to a bass or blue and ask, "Why did you eat that lure?"

The answers can only be guessed, but they might also be surprising. Lure designers spend a lot of time trying to think like a fish and to make their lures swim "just like the real thing." The process of building action into lures is a never-ending quest as lure makers continually try to tweak their creations and improve their fish-catching success.

Lure actions are of several types; fast vibrating, slow pulsating, fast or slow wobbling, and the "do-nothing" lure that has little action or no action at all. Fast vibrating lures like the Rat-L-Trap and some plastic-lip swimmers vibrate rapidly and emit vibrations that travel quite far in the water, and gamefish react aggressively to these dinner-bell sounds, which are easily picked up by the extremely sensitive lateral line nerves of bluefish and striped bass. Tube lures are good examples of slow pulsating lures, while spoons can be fast or slow wobbling type lures. Bucktails have no inherent action of their own, and rely on the angler or the boat's natural rocking motion to breathe life into them.

Why one type of lure action will out-catch another is often beyond accurate explanation, but as fishermen we must recognize that lure actions do influence fish reactions. If what you are trolling is getting no response, it might pay to change to a radically different action, such as switching from a slow tube to a fast vibrating swimmer.

SWIMMING PLUGS

Fishermen began carving wooden plugs to fool freshwater and inshore saltwater fish by the late 1800s, and by the turn of the century the art of plug making was firmly established. My personal antique lure collection includes some amazing metal lures, hollow and soldered at the seams, and some crude hand-carved, hand-painted creations. Today's lure makers have the advantage of superb machinery to assist the carving process, and have developed plug making into an art form with lifelike colors, superb swimming actions and beautiful epoxy finishes that gleam.

Some of these creations are so beautiful that anglers are reluctant to fish them for fear of losing or scratching them! Striped bass fanatics will fish their best wooden plugs only when they are reasonably sure bluefish are not in the local area, such as in late October and November, to minimize the risk to their favorite plugs. Bluefish have no respect for art, and chew right through epoxy finishes, destroying the wood beneath.

Thanks to modern injection molding technology, swimming plugs are constructed of plastic and can be duplicated in large quantities. This brings the price down and also assures high-quality lures that are identical from lure to lure. Molded lures can also be constructed with special chambers that hold metal balls to emit sounds when the lure is trolled. Atom Lures uses a special compaction process to create plastic lure bodies under great pressure that imitate the quality of wooden plugs with the benefits of plastics.

The very best swimming plugs usually have a combination of a side-to-side wiggle enhanced with a rolling action that makes the plug flash. Some derive their swimming actions from molded-in plastic lips, while others rely on the more traditional metal lip. Lures with a long, wide swimming lip will usually dive deeper than a lure with a short lip. A plug's swimming action can be altered slightly by bending the attachment eye up or down. A slight tune-up

Big wooden plugs have been catching striped bass for over 50 years and are still a favorite lure, especially for night fishing.

to bend the eye up will help it dive more deeply. Be careful when fine tuning plugs, because too much alteration and bending may completely ruin the action.

Through-wire construction is an absolute must. All the very best plugs are through-wired, that is, they are constructed with a stainless wire that runs completely through the center of the plug from front to back to which are attached the tail hook, mid-body treble hook and the lure attachment eye that clips to the snap at the end of the line. With through-wire construction, even if the plug breaks, as might happen with a plastic plug, the fish will not be lost because the hooks remain attached to the internal wire.

A tackle rep for a lure manufacturer joined me for a striper trip many years ago and wanted to try for a nice bass on one of the company's new lures. They looked good and swam great, but three 20-pound bass in a row destroyed three plugs one after the other. All that was left was the large plastic swimming lip; the plugs were gone and so were the bass. Back to the drawing board, and a year later with through-wire construction, we played the same game, but this time landed every bass we hooked, including a fat 39 pounder.

TIME-TESTED SPOONS

Today's modern spoons trace their roots back to hand-carved lures made from whalebones or deer antlers. The so-called "turkey bone" trolling lures so popular from the 1920s to the 1950s are beautiful to behold with seductive wobbling actions that bluefish and school bluefin found hard to resist. Metal stamped spoons were much easier to manufacture and replaced bone lures many years ago. Traditional spoons like the Hopkins, Acetta Pet, Clark Squid Spoon and Huntington Drone are just as good today as they were when first designed a half century or more ago. Striped bass and bluefish seem to favor these spoons in sizes from 4 to 9 inches in length, fished singly at the end of a wire trace for blues, a fluorocarbon or mono leader for bass. Although some success had been achieved with free-swinging treble hooks, most spoons utilize a single fixed hook.

Trolling big bluefish off Oregon Inlet, North Carolina on spoons trolled on planer rigs.

Acetta and Crippled Herring manufacture jumbo versions of their standard spoons and they are popular with striped bass trollers in the Chesapeake Bay area, but the grand daddy of big spoons is the famous Montauk Bunker Spoon. From Montauk to central Jersey, these huge spoons have taken countless big striped bass and are a favorite of trollers that specialize in catching the biggest bass of each season. The Wil-Arm spoon is still popular in the Raritan Bay/Sandy Hook regions as is the Reliable bunker spoon originally developed by the now defunct Lupo Lures. Montauk-based charter skipper Jimmy George has mastered the art of spoon making with amazing success with several 60-pound class bass having fallen for his enormous bunker spoons within the shadow of Long Island's famous lighthouse.

BASIC BUCKTAILS

Tie on a leadhead with white bucktail, add a strip of pork rind and you have one of the finest striped bass lures ever devised. A favorite for many years was the Upperman coin-shape bucktail, so was the split-mouth Smilin' Bill, which because of its heavier mass and large head could plumb the depths better than any other bucktail. The SPRO Prime bucktail is one of the most popular of the modern bucktails. The traditional two best colors are all white and all yellow, sometimes spruced up with a red head or a dash of red at the mouth of the Smilin' Bill, but the latest bucktails use a lot more imagination and add color combinations of bucktail hair and synthetic fibers that imitate virtually any baitfish. Chartreuse, pink and purple are popular especially in color schemes that add a white belly, shades of olive and blue on the sides and plenty of flashy Mylar fibers.

Soft-plastic tails fished on leadheads are another excellent bucktail-style lure. Although they lack hair, plastic tails add new dimensions of action with molded paddle or curly tails that wiggle and send out vibrations that fish readily feel and pick up. They also add an enormous array of colors and sizes to perfectly match the size and silhouette of local baitfish.

Parachute bucktails with bucktail or synthetic fibers tied to extend forward and back from the leadhead look like pulsating squid when trolled. The boat's natural rocking action as it bobs with the waves provides some basic action, but parachute jigs are best trolled on a short rod and jigged by the angler working the rod in

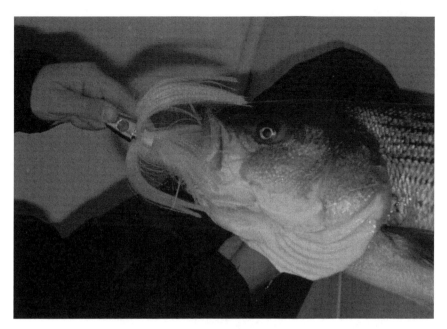

Parachute bucktails trolled on wire line are jigged on short rods to catch bluefish and bass with arm-jolting strikes. Their pulsating nylon skirts look like live squid.

rhythmic sweeps to attract strikes. It's hard work, but the rewards can be well worth it, and there is the added excitement of feeling the jolting strike of a big bluefish or striped bass as it hammers the jig. For best results, parachutes are always fished with a strip of pork rind for maximum action. The pork strips are durable, withstand numerous bluefish strikes and add the advantages of color and action.

Swim shads are similar to leadheads with a plastic tail, but with the plastic molded around the lead weight. This allows greater variety of actions, some of which are ideal for trolling. The largest swim shads can be trolled as single lures or as the center trailer dropped back off an umbrella or shad rig. Aside from their lifelike shape, swim shads are marketed in colors that are so realistic a live bunker would mistake them for a cousin. For trolling, however, I've usually done better with pearl white, chartreuse and pink colors because of their excellent visibility. Some swim shads offer the additional attraction of molded-in holographic panels that flash beautifully.

HOT HOOCHIES

Also called nylons because they are tied with synthetic nylon hair, the generic term hoochie refers to any long nylon lure, usually with a bucktail-style leadhead, and with a 6- to 10-inch length of bead chain or sash weight chain under the nylon hair skirt, which typically measures from 6 to 12 inches in length. Although they have little built-in action, they are deadly on spring bluefish and have been employed by New York and New Jersey charter fleets for decades. Their popularity is enhanced because of their ability to withstand repeated strikes from toothy bluefish and they enjoy a great reputation as a "sure bet" bluefish catcher.

Favorite colors include red/white, blue/white, all white, lime green and all yellow. Imitating their close cousins the bucktail, the natural rocking action of the boat as it rides the waves gives the lures a slow undulating, pulsating action that probably resembles an eel, and bluefish have a tough time saying "No" to a hoochie, especially in the spring when blues are usually traveling in the warmer surface layer of water. Hoochies are most often fished off straight mono near the surface, or from planers to get deep, but they can also be fished off wire line and downriggers.

TUBE LURES

Constructed of soft latex surgical tubing or harder clear nylon tubing, tube lures imitate eels and they are a traditional favorite striped bass lure from New England to Chesapeake Bay. It's easy to duplicate almost any size eel by using small, medium or large diameter tubing, and they can be cut long or short to duplicate the length of any bait.

Striped bass tubes are usually made of the softer surge tube, rather than the harder plastic tubes that are favored for bluefish. Tube lures get their action from the natural curve of the tubing itself, or from a soft wire run through the tube that can be bent to any swimming shape. To get a good swimming action from a natural tube, store them curved. In between fishing trips they can be kept in mesh bags that are popular with offshore fishermen for tuna and marlin lures, or in small Tupperware or Rubbermaid containers. When I make tubes each winter, I store them in large coffee cans near the furnace in the basement so the slight ambient heat helps the tubes take a set, and they retain a nice curved shape. When trolled, the tubes have a slow, undulating swimming action that is deadly.

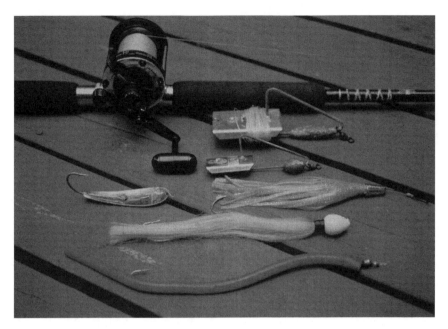

Time-tested bluefish lures include vinyl skirts, nylon-skirted hoochies, tubes and spoons. They can be fished with wire, planers or a downrigger.

Another way to build action into these lures is with a length of wire run down the tube, connecting to a barrel swivel at the head end and the hook at the tail end. The wire can be bent to any shape to make the tube swim with a gentle or aggressive action. Bluefish tend to like the more wild action while striped bass react better to a slow swimming action. One handy way to make wire tubes swim is to wrap, or twist the tube around a short length of broom handle.

One of my biggest bass fell to a giant tube eel. I religiously trolled that 30-inch wine-red lure again and again but failed to take another big fish on it. I've done much better with medium-size tubes of $\frac{3}{8}$-, $\frac{7}{16}$- and $\frac{9}{16}$-inch diameter, in lengths of 12 to 24 inches. Favorite colors include purple, deep red, bright red, dark green, bright green and black.

Manufacturers offer tubes in a wide variety of configurations, including single tubes, jointed tubes and tubes with lead swimming heads for added action. Since tubes do spin, many fishermen like to have a quality barrel swivel at the head end of the lure to avoid line twist.

In New England, tubes are often fished with a sandworm draped on the hook at the tail end of the tube, and trolled slowly on wire line. This tube-and-worm combo is extremely effective, and it works equally well along other coastal locations.

UMBRELLA AND SHAD RIGS

When umbrella rigs first came on the scene about 40 years ago, they were originally armed with short surgical tube lures. Short tubes of 6 to 9 inches were attached to the ends of each arm of the rig, and a longer tube was attached at the center, usually on a drop-back leader of 24 to 48 inches. Although heavy, and with a lot of water resistance when trolled, they caught striped bass like no other lure preceding them. They also caught bluefish, often several at a time, and this ability to catch multiple hook-ups gave umbrella rigs a bad rap in the eyes of some anglers. In the opinion of light-tackle fans, only "meat" fishermen used umbrella rigs.

While multiple hook-ups can be a common occurrence, there is also no dispute that large bass in early spring and late fall would also strike an umbrella rig, and 99 percent of the time they would strike and get hooked by the trailing center tube or shad. To savvy striped bass trollers looking for giant bass, umbrella rigs have gained a reliable reputation as a big-fish lure, and that's a good reason to make them part of your own lure arsenal.

Umbrella rigs armed with bright tubes or spoons will attract bluefish from spring through fall, and the soft, but resilient, tubes are able to withstand repeated strikes and hook-ups with toothy bluefish. A slow trolling speed will get more attention from striped bass, but kick up the engine rpms another 100 turns and the slightly faster speed will get plenty of hook-ups from bluefish.

The latest umbrella rigs have morphed into what trollers now call shad rigs. Surge tubes have given way to soft-plastic shad bodies rigged on short mono leaders. Although shad rigs are even heavier and more resistant than traditional umbrella rigs, they offer several advantages, such as a wide variety of colors, sizes, profiles and swimming tails with a terrific action. Shad rigs are amazingly lifelike in appearance and are responsible for catching large numbers of striped bass in spring and fall. You do not want to troll them when too many bluefish are around, such as in the summer months, because ol' yellow eye will destroy the plastic shads.

Launching an umbrella rig in a pendulum swing assures a tangle-free entry into the water.

For the maximum flash appeal, umbrella rigs can be rigged with small spoons at the end of each arm, and when rigged this way, they are superb bluefish lures. The small spoons must be rigged on short 60- to 80-pound mono leaders with a barrel swivel at the top of the short leader, which then attaches to the umbrella rig arm. Without the swivel, the leaders will twist and coil badly and the lure will not catch fish. A single spoon can also be used as a center drop back and will effectively catch striped bass and bluefish.

Another excellent drop-back lure is a large swimming plug, but not a deep-diving plug. A shallow-running plug is preferred because the weight of the umbrella rig, or the length of wire line, or the downrigger will take the umbrella to the required trolling depth. A big plug at the tail end of an umbrella on an 80-pound length of leader has paid off handsomely for many striped bass trollers. Be sure the hooks are large, and that they are at least 3X strong, or you may lose some big striped bass. These are powerful fish that can straighten wimpy hooks.

Soft plastic shads are fished on short mono leaders clipped to the arms of umbrella rigs and look like a school of baitfish. Chartreuse, pearl, blue and white and purple are usually the hot colors.

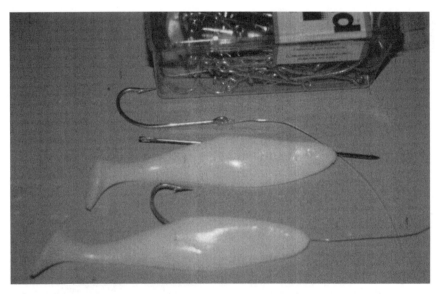

Use a stainless steel rigging needle to quickly rig a supply of shads. Tie the hook to a 12-inch length of 60-pound mono; push the rigging needle through the shad, pulling the leader with it until the hook is seated. A barrel swivel finishes off the leader.

Whether you arm an umbrella rig with tubes, shads or spoons, extra action can be achieved by adding mono leaders between the lure and the umbrella rig arm. The leaders can all be of the same length, or they can be varied so that one lure is dropped back 12 inches, another at 18, a third at 30 inches and a fourth at 36 inches. The center lure can be dropped back anywhere from 30 to 60 inches.

Leaders can be made up ahead of time in various lengths and stored in tubes to keep them straight, and then clipped to the tubes as needed, or stored coiled in Tupperware containers, Ziploc bags or leader bags like the type sold in tackle shops. Remember to stretch a coiled leader before using it so it lays straight. A Duolock snap at one-end clips to the lure, a barrel swivel at the other end clips to the end of the umbrella rig arm. If you want less hardware, tie the tube or shad directly to the leader, but use the same barrel swivel arrangement to snap the lure to the umbrella rig arm. Leaders for the center, or drop-back, lure can be made up, and stored, in the same manner.

Getting an umbrella rig into the water without tangling all the tubes or shads can be tricky unless you "launch" the rig properly. If the umbrella rig is simply dropped into the water, the tubes and shads will turn backward as they hit the water and tangle around the main leader, the short lure leaders or the arms of the rig itself making quite a mess. The fouled lure will not look realistic and will most likely go fishless.

To launch an umbrella rig, reel the rig to within a few inches of the rod tip, keep your thumb on the spool and engage the reel's clicker. Point the rod at a 45 degree angle away from the transom and keep the rod tip low to the water. With the boat in gear and moving forward, swing the rod tip forward in an arc so the umbrella rig moves like a pendulum and plunges into the water with tubes or shads swinging behind it. Immediately free-spool the reel and allow about 25 feet of line to stream from the spool. Stop the line with thumb pressure, and with the rod tip pointed at the water, take a close look at the rig to be sure no tubes or shads are tangled, and then continue to stream line until the lure is at the proper depth.

The pendulum swing is easy to master and makes deploying an umbrella rig a very simple chore. As the lure plunges into the water, the natural resistance of the water keeps pressure on the tubes or shads soothe remain tangle free. The pendulum swings works equally well with wire line, lead core, mono or braid.

CHAPTER 3

Trolling with Mono

Trolling with monofilament line is a good choice when gamefish are positioned near the surface, or when the water is shallow. Monofilament lines have a larger diameter than braided super lines, and when compared to wire line, monofilament has virtually no weight. Its relatively large diameter has a lot of water resistance when trolled as the water pushes against the line. This lifting force of the water applied along, let's say, a 200-foot length of mono is quite substantial and causes the line to kite or rise in the water. This can be a big advantage when trying to keep lures near the surface when trolling in shallow water, or when only the surface water temperature is comfortable for gamefish.

This characteristic is a big advantage during the spring run of bluefish when the fish are swimming north and holding in the warmest top 10 feet of water. A deep-diving lure or a wire line setup would travel well below the fish and achieve few strikes or hook-ups. A similar situation occurs when striped bass are holding in shallow water over a reef, bar, shoal or along the beachfront in 15 to 20 feet of water or less. In this shallow-water situation monofilament line performs beautifully.

Many back-bay situations are also perfect for trolling small lures on mono when striped bass or bluefish are holding along channel edges, shoals and flats areas. This trolling technique is used to locate the fish, which when found, can then be cast to, or the angler can continue to troll.

There are many monofilament lines from which to choose, and each has attributes that can help catch more fish. Monofilament lines are made up of nylon chemical formulations called polymers. To a chemist, the term monofilament technically belongs to a single polymer line formulation, but many of today's lines are blends of several polymers, often called copolymer lines. Since they all have the same basic look and feel, for the sake of a fishing discussion, we'll call them all "monofilament" lines. There are some significant differences, however, between one fishing line and another that can enhance your fishing success.

Many copolymer lines generally have a harder, slicker outer surface when compared to a single polymer line, and this feature makes them more abrasion resistant. All mono lines stretch to some extent, but some considerably more than others. Manufacturers have recently begun marketing mono lines with low stretch, a quality that is very important in a trolling line. Many original mono lines stretched as much as 25 to 30 percent of their length before breaking. The lines acted like long rubber bands and it was often difficult to set the hook. While working the rod and reel in a pumping motion to gain line, it was difficult to get line back on the reel quickly because when the rod tip was lifted 3 to 4 feet to gain line; the line simply stretched and got longer. In reality, only a few inches of line would be retrieved and cranked back onto the reel.

Seasoned trollers have mixed opinions about line diameter. A line with a robust diameter is easier to handle while fishing and when tying knots, especially at night, but less line can be packed onto the reel spool. Traditions die hard and many fishermen still prefer a tough, thick line. Small line nicks, or line chafing will weaken the line less than those same problems do with a thin diameter line.

Special copolymer lines with a hard, tough outer shell allow thin diameter lines to compete very well against large diameter lines in the abrasion resistance department. Thin diameter lines are a good choice when you want additional line capacity, or want to use lighter, more compact tackle. There's a significant and growing trend today to use smaller, lighter tackle for all types of fishing and this includes trolling. A slim-diameter line will allow more line to be packed onto a small reel. The lighter reel is handier to use and adds a big dose of sport to the day's fishing. Because the tackle is lighter, fishing is more fun.

Line color has become more important in recent years. My personal preference is for the hi-vis bright yellow lines because they are much easier to see, even in bright sunlight, compared to a line with no color. When trolling, much of the line is in the air between the rod tip and the water where the fish can't see it. The length of line in the water will always have a clear leader at the end so; again, the fish can't see it. The important thing is that the angler can see the line and keep track of it while maneuvering the boat to make turns and work the trolling pattern. A hi-vis line erases all doubt about where the line is so the skipper can handle the boat with more confidence. Traditionalists will choose a less visible line, such as clear, blue, green or the time-tested pink.

Before purchasing a monofilament line, it can pay off with more fish later if you take the time to carefully research several brands so you can select the best line with all the properties you need. While color and line diameter are more of a convenience quality for the angler, the choice of a low-stretch line is helpful for trolling.

TACKLE CHOICES

Conventional tackle is the most popular trolling tackle, although there are some applications where spinning gear can be used, such as in light-tackle back-bay trolling. Fishermen often use ambiguous terms like "heavy" and "light" to describe their tackle choices, but we need to be more specific to make the best choices.

Reels can be either the star-drag or lever-drag type. Rod choices focus on rod length, and the action and power of the rod blank. The type of guides and hardware is also important, and the size of the fish needs to be considered. A pool cue isn't needed for school stripers, but a light-action wimpy rod will never work when trolling spoons off planers for bluefish, or when big bass are the quarry. So let's take a look at what works best.

Back bay or river fishing for school-size stripers and spring bluefish can easily be accomplished with a wide-spool conventional, level-wind reel filled with 250 yards of 12- to 15-pound test mono and matched to a fast-taper rod of 6½ to 7 feet in length. A perennial favorite reel choice is the Ambassadeur 6000-size, and there are dozens of similar reels from other manufacturers, some with graphite frames, and the best with machined aluminum frames.

Monofilament line is a good choice for shallow-water trolling, but with deep-diving plugs it can also plumb the depths for big bluefish and stripers.

Foam grips are considered more comfortable to hold onto when hands are wet, but cork grips are more sensitive and give the angler a better "feel" of the lure and the line. A gimbal nock at the butt of the rod is helpful to keep the rod and reel positioned correctly in the rod holder. Most anglers prefer conventional gear, but spinning tackle is acceptable if it can handle the same pound-test line.

Inshore trolling tackle choices depend on several variables: size of the fish and their location, type of lure and whether a planer will be used. The reel can be either a star-drag or a lever-drag type. For shallow-running sub-surface lures such as spoons, tubes, shallow-running swimmers, bucktails and swim shads, a conventional rod and reel combination capable of handling 350 yards of 20- to 30-pound line is about right. The Penn GTi 320LD, Quantum Cabo PTs 20, Okuma Catalina and Shimano Tekota are good examples of reels for most inshore trolling. Many are available with a levelwind feature and some are marketed in line counter versions, an option that many trollers like to keep track of the amount of line being trolled.

A 6½ or 7-foot rod with a stout butt section and sensitive tip is preferred, and it's a good idea to avoid a rod with an extremely fast taper action. The Fuji heavy-duty silicone nitride guides are recommended, a gimbal is a must and a slick butt will aid removal from the rod holder when a big bass is yanking hard on the line.

For deep-diving plugs and planers, both of which have a tremendous amount of pull, a stout rod is a must. Charter skippers favor 30-pound mono and a reel with lots of retrieve power. A Shimano TLD 15, Okuma Convector or a Penn 330GTi would be good choices in the reel department, matched to a rod like the Lamiglas BL7030W or the St. Croix SWC66MF.

RIGGING UP

Because making connections with monofilament is so easy, rigging a mono trolling setup is simple and quick. Depending on the pound test of the main fishing line, you may not even need a leader.

I like to have complete control over my tackle, even from the initial rigging stages, so I prefer to pack the line on the reel myself. I can make sure the mono is placed on the spool carefully with an evenly spaced side-to-side guiding of the line. If the line is installed with an aggressive crisscrossing, it's possible to get a severe case of line rash later when fighting a big fish under a heavy drag setting. The crackling sound as the line rubs against itself as it comes off the spool is a clear warning that a problem is occurring. Line rash can also occur when the reel is filled with fresh line coming off the service spool at an extreme criss-crossing angle.

I also want to know that the line is firmly and evenly packed on the spool. Loosely packed line will be a problem later when you are actually fighting a fish. As the fish pulls line, it does so with a lot of tension and the tight line will dig into the underlying coils and jam. The tight coils may also jam up the next time you let out the line. The tight line wound onto the reel under pressure of fighting a fish may cause a very big problem with the tight line digging into the loose coils and causing a horrible line snarl or tangle.

A leader at the terminal end is helpful. The extra measure of safety that protects against cut-offs caused by the line chafing against the bottom of the boat or an outboard engine when the fish is at boat side, or from scrapping in the net, is valuable insurance. A heavy leader also makes boating fish easy by allowing the mate or a crewmember to take a wrap on the leader with a gloved hand

and then swing the fish over the cover boards. This works very well with fish of less than 10 to 15 pounds.

A leader can be added in several ways. The simplest method uses a barrel swivel between the main line and the leader, tied in place with an improved clinch at the leader and a double uni-knot at the line. A more sophisticated leader system uses a short double line created by tying a Bimini twist or Spider hitch at the end of the main line, then add the heavier leader with a surgeon's knot or opposing uni-knots. These knots are covered in detail at the tag end of this book.

At the end of the leader, use a Palomar or improved clinch knot to attach the snap or snap swivel. I like to slip a small plastic bead onto the leader before tying on the snap. The small bead acts as a protective cushion whenever the snap is reeled to the rod tip, which may help avoid a broken tip-top.

A simple snap is preferred when pulling lures that do not spin, such as plugs, bucktails and shads, but a snap swivel is mandatory when tubes and spoons are used to avoid severe line twist. When choosing a snap or snap swivel, select the smallest size that exceeds the strength of the leader. The goal is to balance the tackle at every opportunity and a snap swivel rated at 200-pound test on a 30-pound leader is overkill. SPRO, Sea Striker and others make exceptionally strong, but small snaps and snap swivels that are a better choice. The swivels are less visible to the fish and are better balanced with the overall tackle.

TROLLING DRAILS

Monofilament will take spoons, nylons, bucktails, swim shads, shallow-swimming plugs and tube lures in the depth range of 5 to 15 feet. Lures with deep-diving lips will go deeper. Additional depth can be achieved by adding a 2- to 8-ounce torpedo-shape trolling drail at the end of the line. For each 4 ounces of drail weight, an additional trolling depth of 5 feet will be gained. When employing a trolling weight, it's best to add a 10- to 15-foot leader between the drail and the lure.

Drails are available in sizes that range from only a half-ounce on up to jumbo 16-ounce weights. Some have bead chain run through the center, others have only an attachment eye at each end, while others have a fin-shape appendage to help them track straight and to help reduce any potential for twisting, and still others have a snap swivel at one end.

My preference is to keep the drail setup as strong as possible, so I use a "Plain Jane" drail with through-wire construction and only an attachment eye at each end. For maximum strength I tie the lure leader to the drail with a double improved clinch knot for leaders of less than 30-pound test, and a three-turn improved clinch for leaders of 30-pound test and above.

Leader length from the drail to the lure is usually 10 to 15 feet, although in some extreme situations when fish are very spooky 20 feet may be required. The disadvantage of a long leader is need to handline the fish to the boat once the drail is at the rod tip.

TROLLING PLANERS

It wasn't long after the War for Southern Independence was settled that sail-powered skiffs were trolling for bluefish in Long Island Sound and along the Jersey Coast with metal devices that eventually evolved into the modern planer. Originally called trolling sleds, they used a weighted nose and metal diving wing that could "fly" the lure down the depths. Since the 1930s, planers have been a standard for charter boats seeking bluefish in the spring, and they are still employed by many boats today.

A feisty spring bluefish is welcomed aboard after taking a flashy spoon lure trolled off a planer along a coastal inshore ridge.

Traditional modern planers are constructed of lead and stainless steel and are virtually indestructible. A lead nose weight and a stainless steel wing are mounted on a stainless steel wire frame. They are simple to use, relatively inexpensive, and can take a lure trolled on monofilament down to depths of 20 to 40 feet. A planer can be added to the end of the main fishing line quickly whenever you find yourself in a situation where the fish have sounded, or you have no alternate way to go deep, such as with wire line, a downrigger or with deep-diving plugs.

Although a growing number of deep trollers have switched to downriggers, there's still a strong contingent of traditionalist trollers that like to pull planers for spring and early summer bluefish. The tackle is easy to set up, and depending on the size of the planer, depths of 15 to 30 feet are attainable.

There is no standardized size numbering system for planers, but the smallest sizes are usually marked as size OO or size 1, and the numbers go up as the planer size increases. For private boat use, the Sea Striker size 2, 3 and 4 planers are generally preferred and they will run at depths of about 20 feet.

Luhr-Jensen makes several high-impact plastic planers, some with adjustable blades to allow the planer to ride to the left or right, which helps keep the lures apart while trolling. Although several styles are available, Luhr-Jensen's Pink Lady is the most popular with saltwater trollers.

Planers are attached directly to the main fishing line by using a large size 56 Duolock snap clipped to the brass ring, which slides along the sturdy stainless steel wire frame. When slack is placed in the fishing line, the lead nose weight angles the planer downward and the brass attachment ring slides to the rear of the frame. This position "arms" the planer so the wing can maintain its diving angle. When a fish strikes and pulls on the leader, the brass ring slides forward, which "disarms" the planer so it, and the fish, can be reeled in.

The lure is attached to the tail end of the planer via a 30- to 60-pound mono leader, usually about 15 to 20 feet in length. When reeling a fish, once the planer reaches the rod tip, the leader must be handlined to get the fish into the boat, which some trollers consider a detraction. In actual practice, however, gathering the leader takes only a few moments, and it is easily accomplished. When bluefish are extremely aggressive, the leader length may be shortened to only 10 feet, but it is best to start out with a longer leader to keep the planer away from the lure and avoid spooking wary fish.

This planer shows the "armed" and ready position. The lure is trolled on a 15-foot leader off the back of the planer. The planer's diving wing digs deep into the water column.

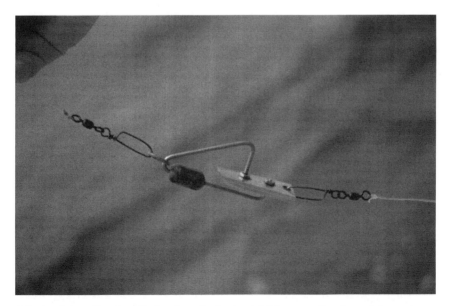

When a fish strikes, it pulls hard on the leader, which causes the ring and snap to slide forward "disarming" the planer so the angler can fight the fish unhindered.

Setting a planer into the trolling pattern is easy. Free spool the reel until the lure, planer and appropriate amount of line (about 75 feet) is set out behind the boat. Lift the rod tip to vertical, then quickly drop the tip toward the water, then lift it at a 45-degree angle. The momentary slack line allows the lead nose to set the diving angle, the brass ring slides back on the wire frame and the planer is armed and ready to troll.

DEEP-DIVING PLUGS

Mann's Bait Company set the striped bass and bluefish trolling world on its ear when it introduced the now-famous Stretch series of plastic-lipped, deep-diving plugs. Finally, a lure could be trolled at great depths without need of wire, downriggers, lead core, heavy trolling drails or planers. After careful research, Mann's designed lures that could run at predictable depths and marketed their lures as the Stretch series with the lure's depth as part of the name; Stretch 12, Stretch 20 and on up to the huge Stretch Giganticus G-50.

Other manufacturers followed and today there is a wide array of lure sizes, colors, actions and variations from which to select, including deep divers with hard-plastic bodies and soft-plastic tails that are so lifelike, a real eel would fall in love with them. The best lures are of high quality with rugged and dependable through-wire construction and lips that even a whack with a hammer can't destroy, and the plugs should be equipped with 3X-strong treble hooks.

The manufacturer's trolling depths will vary with the speed of the boat and the amount of line let out. With mono's tendency to kite, the deep lures can actually be lifted slightly and won't run as deep if too much line is let out. I've had the most consistent results with about 100 feet of line paid out. I mark my mono with a permanent-ink Magic Marker pen at 75, 100 and 150 feet and use these reference marks to fine tune the amount of trolling line.

One word of caution; when retrieving deep divers, as the plug nears the surface it is a good idea to hold the rod tip down toward the water and angled at 45 degrees away from the transom. When the plug pops free of the water, it can fly at you like it was shot from a cannon. If the rod is held pointing up to the sky and straight in line with the angler, when the lure pops free, it will be on a path directly at the angler's head, which is not a happy position to be in.

When rigging tackle for deep-diving plugs, many trollers prefer a straight connection to the lure with no leader, only a large snap at the terminal end, but I feel the leader is helpful, especially for controlling the fish at the side of the boat because the leader provides something beefier to grab hold of.

It's easy to collect a wide array of deep divers to cover every depth from 12 to 40 feet, plus a variety of colors. They don't fit handily into most tackle boxes, so innovative anglers, like Bob Kamienksi of the Hi-Mar Striper Club, store their deep divers in plastic tubes. They cut a clear plastic tube like the type sold to protect fluorescent light bulbs to whatever length is needed for their plugs. A Snapple iced tea bottle cap is just the right size to press snugly into the tube to form a bottom. The tubes can then be stored into the ever-handy 5-gallon plastic bucket for easy carrying to the boat.

CHAPTER 4

Trolling with Super-Braid Lines

Trolling with super-braid lines for striped bass and bluefish is rapidly gaining in popularity along some stretches of the inshore East Coast. It's easy to use, requires no special tackle, and it can be used for surface trolling and for deep trolling. Deep trolling? Before you think I've lost my marbles, keep an open mind and be ready to do some experimenting. The rewards of fishing with super-braid lines to take lures deep can be exceptionally rewarding.

Like wire line, super-braid lines have no discernable stretch, so you feel the fight of the fish with a sensitivity that is remarkable. Unlike wire, super braids are virtually weightless so the tackle can be scaled down for a more pleasurable angling experience while fighting the fish. By substituting braid for wire, and a smaller reel, the troller can trim a lot of weight from the rod and reel tackle package.

Unlike monofilament, super lines have extremely small line diameters with exceptional line strength. A super braid of 50- to 80-pound test has a diameter similar to 12- or 15-pound test mono. This fine diameter allows super-braid lines to literally slice through the water like a knife and with reduced line resistance in the water, braided lines take lures deeper than monofilament, and almost as deep as wire line. With a 3- or 6-ounce lure, such as a heavy buck-tail or an umbrella rig, super-braid lines will run at almost the same depth as a 150-foot length of wire line, which is about 15 to 20 feet below the surface.

TACKLE CHOICES

My first efforts with super-braid lines for deep trolling used a Shimano TLD-20 filled with 200 yards of 60-pound monofilament backing under a top shot of 150 yards of 50-pound white super braid. Since then, I've gone to reels that are smaller in size and lighter in weight, and I don't bother with the monofilament backing. There are many good candidates, such as the Shimano Trinidad 20, Quantum Cabo CLW30, Okuma Catalina and Penn GTi 320 LD. My favorite outfit lately has been the Penn International 975 CSLD matched to a rod with a sensitive tip and a powerful butt section, like the Lamiglas BL7030W. This rod and reel combination provides plenty of versatility, power and sensitivity for efficient fishing.

Some anglers have used lighter 30-pound test braid to gain added line capacity or to further downsize the reel size. Using 30-pound braid with its slightly smaller line diameter allows you to drop down one reel size, such as substituting a Trinidad 16 for the Trinidad 20, without sacrificing any line capacity, and to also use a lighter rod, however, this is only adequate for small- to medium-size stripers and bluefish. Hang a 30- to 40-pound striped bass and you'll want the added power and insurance of beefier tackle.

Spring bluefish are a great opportunity to scale down tackle and go light. These fish cruise about 15 feet below the surface, so letting out approximately 200 feet of super braid will allow you to consistently make good catches of blues. Best of all, you can scale down your tackle and use a rod and reel that is barely heavier than deep-water fluking tackle. I've been using an Ambassadeur C4 6600 filled with 20-pound braid and a light conventional rod designed to handle 20-pound line. This outfit is a lot of fun when fishing the braid with a 4-ounce drail at the end of the main fishing line, an 8-foot mono leader and a size 3½ Huntington Drone spoon. What a pleasure to catch these 5- to 10-pound fish on light tackle!

When choosing a braided line, it must be balanced realistically to the rod and reel, and it must be comfortable to fish with. Most braided lines are labeled for their own inherent pound test, and for the pound test of the equivalent diameter of monofilament. For instance, 20-pound braid has the same approximate diameter as 6-pound mono; 50-pound braid is similar in diameter to 12- or 15-pound mono. When trolling for big bass and with large lures, even though the 20-pound braid is strong enough to do the job, it is not so thin that working with it becomes a challenge. I try to find a middle ground that balances line diameter and strength, and which I feel is comfortable to handle and easy to spool on the reel.

Trolling with super-braid lines is a viable alternative to wire line fishing, and is especially popular when trolling deep-diving plugs. Fishermen appreciate the light weight of the braided trolling rod and reel, which is substantially lighter than a wire line outfit.

As a general rule of thumb, I match the braided line to a reel so that it holds a bit more line than the equivalent pound-test line capacity for mono. For instance, on a reel that would usually hold 300 yards of 15-pound mono, I'd probably be able to get 450 or more yards of 30-pound braid, or about 375 yards of 50-pound test braid. For heavy duty trolling, the 50-pound braid is much handier to use than the 30 pound, but for medium trolling, such as for school and mid-size stripers, or when using lighter lures, the 30 is just fine. In some light-tackle situations, 20-pound braid can be used.

Braid is more expensive than mono, and for this reason many anglers use mono backing and then add a less costly top-shot of 150 to 300 yards of braid. This works well, but I prefer to use all braid so there are no connections to worry about. To minimize expense, I reverse the braided line at the end of the season by spooling the line onto an empty bulk spool, then transferring it again to another empty bulk spool, then back onto the reel. The underlying line of last year is now the fresh new line of this year. It's an easy mid-winter chore, and with an electric drill and a threaded 5-inch long, ¼-inch diameter bolt to hold the empty bulk spools, it takes only about ten minutes per reel. It saves a few bucks to spend on other fishing tackle.

If you use mono backing, it's a good idea to install backing that is rated at one pound-test heavier than the braid. If a big fish takes all the braid, you don't want to risk losing the fish, the lure and the braid to backing that is less strong than the main fishing line. For instance, when using 30-pound test braid as the main line, use 40-pound test backing.

Not sure how much backing to use? Here's a trick that works well, although it requires that you use two reels, which you should be doing anyway to match your tackle to the boat—same rod and reel combo on port and starboard while trolling. On reel number one, wind on the 150-yard braided line first, then the backing until the reel is full. Then transfer the line from reel number one to reel number two. As you do so, take note of the spool level when all the backing is on the reel. You can measure this with a small ruler to be very accurate, and when installing the backing back onto reel number one, you'll know exactly how much you need. A small spiral notebook at your workbench is a handy reference for the future when you're not sure how much line you put on the reel last year.

Two of the best super-line attributes are their lack of stretch and smaller diameter. Fishermen can pack more and heavier pound-test line on their reels, which is a good thing if the tackle can stand up to it. Using 50-pound braid on a reel designed to handle 20-pound can place severe strain on gears, handles, drags and bearings that support spools and shafts. Failure of the reel is not the fault of the manufacturer, but of the angler who didn't match the line to the reel. When spooling up with super braid, be sure the reel you use is up to the task. All manufacturers are now making downsized reels that are rugged as a tank and which can easily handle the amazing power of super line.

Rods can also fall victim to super-line abuse. A high-quality blank designed with superior manufacturing technology and the best materials to handle 20-pound line, may not stand up to the rigors demanded by a tight drag and 50-pound super braid. The rod can break, and if it does, it is "pilot error," not a flaw in the manufacturing process of the rod itself. Several manufacturers are designing blanks with added layers of material that combine both fiberglass and graphite to help the rods withstand the enormous stress that super braids can place on tackle. When selecting a rod for trolling with braid, be sure you get one made specifically for super-braid lines.

CALCULATING THE DEPTH RANGE

The key to proper lure presentation is the ability to present the lure at the correct depth so the lure travels past the fish at exactly the same level as they are holding. By marking the braid every 50 feet, just as is done when fishing with wire line, it is an easy task to calculate the exact trolling depth. Most super braids sold on the East Coast are dark green in color and line marks applied with permanent ink are hard to see. These same braided lines, however, are also available in hi-vis yellow, white or pale gray, which are the popular colors on the West Coast and with offshore anglers. If the lighter colors are not available, you may have to convince your local tackle shop to special order the light-color line for you. I've used both white super-braid line and hi-vis yellow and applied 6-inch marks with a permanent-ink Magic Marker pen. I made my marks at 100, 150, 200 and 300 feet.

After several fishing trips, the marks will fade and need to be retouched to be more visible. They can also be color coded with red, blue, green or black to provide a visual reference to help determine how much line is out. As an example, black is 100, blue is 150, red is 200, and green is 250 feet.

If you fish at night, visual marks are useless. Night trollers like to rely on the feel of the marks slipping through their fingers to determine the amount of line needed. A "feel good" mark for night fishing can be made by stretching a small rubber band alongside the braided line and then applying 10 half hitches of dental floss or Gudebrod's Bait Rig'N Floss around the super-braid line and the rubber band. When the tag end of the rubber band is clipped off, the rubber relaxes and is jammed against the overlying wraps of floss and against the braided line so the mark is held tight to the line and completely immovable.

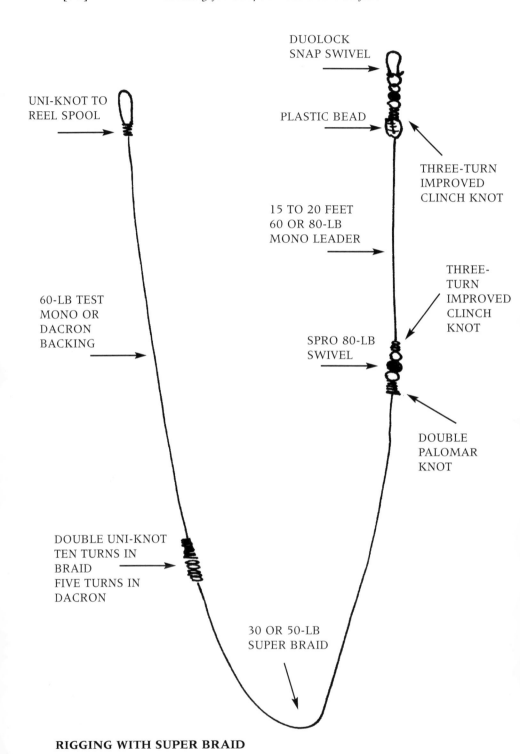

DUOLOCK
SNAP SWIVEL

UNI-KNOT TO
REEL SPOOL

PLASTIC BEAD

THREE-TURN
IMPROVED
CLINCH KNOT

15 TO 20 FEET
60 OR 80-LB
MONO LEADER

THREE-
TURN
IMPROVED
CLINCH
KNOT

60-LB TEST
MONO OR
DACRON
BACKING

SPRO 80-LB
SWIVEL

DOUBLE
PALOMAR
KNOT

DOUBLE UNI-KNOT
TEN TURNS IN
BRAID
FIVE TURNS IN
DACRON

30 OR 50-LB
SUPER BRAID

RIGGING WITH SUPER BRAID

Early experiments showed that for every 50 feet of super braid in the water, not counting the line between the rod tip and the water, approximately 4 feet of trolling depth is achieved when using a 4- to 6-ounce shad rig. To verify this, I trolled parallel to the beach in my home waters off Point Pleasant, New Jersey coast, first angling toward, and then away from, the beach on a zig-zag trolling pattern so the lures traveled over bottom depths ranging from 25 to 40 feet. With 300 feet of super braid in the water, my shad rig hit the bottom when the depth finder read 23 feet—about 4 feet of depth for every 50 feet of line. Adding a 4-ounce drail to the shad rig got me to the 28-foot depth with 300 feet of super braid. This is not dramatically different than trolling with wire line, which usually achieves about 5 feet of depth for every 50 feet of line in the water.

You can verify these results yourself if you have a gently sloping, snag-free sandy bottom somewhere near where you fish. Troll a zig-zag pattern that takes the lures from shallow to deep. You'll see the rod tip bounce and dip when the lures hit the bottom. Your fishfinder will verify the depth, and the marks on the braid tell you how much line is in the water. Multiply the lure depth by 50, and divide the total by the length of line at the water. Based on this simple formula you can predict the approximate lure depth for every 50 feet of line in the water. For instance, let's say your lure hit bottom in 17 feet of water with 200 feet of braid at the water. Multiply 17 by 50, divide by 200 feet and you'll get a depth value of about 4 feet for every 50 feet of line in the water.

Just as when trolling with monofilament line, adding a trolling drail of 4 ounces will gain an additional 5 feet of water depth. An 8-ounce drail will gain 10 additional feet of depth.

By changing the amount of line in the water, and by adding drails, super braid can be effectively used to troll in depths from 12 to 35 feet. Let's look at some typical examples; 150 feet of braid will take the lure to about 12 feet of depth, 250 feet of braid will take the lure to about 20 feet below the surface, and 300 feet of braid with a 4-ounce drail will take the lure to about 30 feet of depth.

It is important to remember that these calculations are approximations based on trolling at about 3 knots. Faster trolling speeds will increase the water pressure on the line causing it to rise and thereby reducing the depth, while a slower speed with its reduced water pressure against the line will increase the depth of the line.

Trolling with the current will allow the lures to go deeper, while trolling against the current will make them rise. Ditto for trolling with or against the wind, with or against a wind-driven surface-water current.

RIGGING UP

There are several backing-to-braid and braid-to-leader connections that have proven reliable and which also provide the strength to handle many fishing situations. How you rig will partially depend upon the lures you pull and the fish you are targeting. Spring blues don't need as heavy a tackle combination as fall's jumbo stripers, and you can rig accordingly.

If you use mono backing beneath a top-shot of 150 to 300 yards of super line, connect the two lines with uni-knots, and be sure to double the braided line. Make five turns of the mono backing, but ten turns of the braid and draw down carefully. Use gloves to get a firm grip on the fine-diameter super line to be sure the knot is snug and neat. For an extra measure of safety and reliability, add a drop of Hard As Nails clear nail polish to the knot connection. This protective coating does not add any significant knot strength, but it does reduce wearing and fraying as the knot repeatedly passes through the rod guides.

When trolling with umbrella rigs or shad rigs, the braid can be tied direct to the snap swivel, which is then clipped to the rig. A double-improved clinch knot is used to attach the snap swivel at the end of the braid.

With a 4-ounce drail, super braid can present a shad rig at about 25 feet below the surface, just right for fall striped bass on inshore hot spots.

Most fishermen, however, will prefer to add a length of mono at the end of the main fishing line. I like to have a 15-foot mono leader and use the super-strong size #6 SPRO barrel swivel rated at 80-pound test between the mono and the super braid. A double-improved clinch knot or a Palomar knot are excellent connections to attach the braided line to the swivel. A three-turn clinch knot attaches the mono leader to the other eye of the swivel. You can also use a swivel to connect the backing to the top shot of braid, using the same knots. The swivels are small enough to easily pass through the rod guides and are extremely reliable.

If you don't like the idea of swivels, no matter how small, running through the rod guides, attach the mono to the super line with uni-knots or a five-turn surgeon's knot. In both cases, double the braided line. A few drops of Hard As Nails will add a protective coating, or use Loon Hard Head clear fly finish. Any fly shop will have it in stock and it's great stuff for coating knots.

DEEP DIVERS

Going deep with big-lipped plastic plugs pulled on super braid has proven to be an effective way to reach big and early summer stripers and blues. Most of what was described in the previous chapter covering trolling with monofilament and deep-diving plugs applies just as well to super-braid lines.

There are several advantages, however, to pulling diving plugs on braid. The line has no stretch so the lure's action is transmitted to the rod tip and the angler can watch the rhythm of the tip to verify the plug is working correctly. The slightest bit of weed will clearly show up as the tip's pulsating action will be affected. The fine diameter of the braid slices through the water with far less resistance than the mono, which allows the lures to run deeper with less line. Braid is very abrasion resistant, and it can withstand a lot of abuse from scrapes against the side of the boat or from the sharp-edged gill plates of striped bass. This is a big plus when tangling with trophy-size striped bass when you do not want to lose the fish of a lifetime because of line failure.

Another advantage of the line's no-stretch personality is the way it enhances the fight of every fish you catch. Every lunge, every head shake is telegraphed directly up the line to the rod and then to the angler's hands. Every nuance of the contest is felt, and, therefore, appreciated. Since the tackle is usually lighter in physical weight, the battle is much more sporting and substantially more enjoyable.

CHAPTER 5

Trolling with Wire Line & Lead Core

The old fisherman's tale that for every fish you find up on top, there are ten more in the deeper water below is probably true. For every rule, there are exceptions; but a check of your fishfinder or colorscope while trolling will usually show more evidence of bait and gamefish below the surface than your eye can see on top. Getting down to these deep fish can be accomplished in several ways, including the time-tested wire-line system and also with lead core line, especially whenever bluefish and striped bass are located at 20 to 40 feet of water.

Keep in mind the most important consideration is fish depth, not necessarily water depth. Wire-line and lead-core trolling will catch fish in water depths of 15 to 40 feet when striped bass are holding close to the bottom; and they also work very well when bass are found in 60 feet of water holding at 25 feet below the surface. This is also very typical of bluefish where they may be holding at a mid-depth range of 20 to 30 feet in water that is 90 feet deep. All these scenarios are perfect for wire line or lead core.

Using wire line or lead core to get lures deep has been a favorite method for trollers from New England south to New Jersey, but is not as popular below Cape May. In Chesapeake Bay wire line again regains popularity, although many skippers there prefer braided stainless steel wire that is more flexible and therefore easier to use than single-strand wire. I like the braided wire, too, and have been using Malin braided stainless steel 40-pound wire with excellent results.

Some anglers feel wire-line fishing is unsporting, but this misconception is probably due to the fact that many wire-line trollers also use umbrella rigs which are cumbersome and have a heavy feel in the water. Fighting a fish on wire is actually a lot more sensitive when compared to mono because unlike monofilament that stretches, wire has virtually no stretch. Set the hook on a trophy-sized striped bass and the fight is amazing as every head shake, every lunge and every vibration is transmitted up the line to the angler. There's no rubber-band effect to cushion the fight as with monofilament.

Trolling with wire line can be challenging and exciting, or arm tiring and very "ho-hum" in between fish strikes. It all depends on whether you're just a winder-grinder, or the driver. The winder-grinder needs lots of patience in between bites, strong arms to reel in all that wire and a mild disposition to put up the skipper's shouts to "Keep reeling!"

The boat driver or skipper, however, needs brainpower, not muscles. He must have a sharp eye and the ability to analyze water conditions, plot courses from one good spot to another, avoid cut-offs from nearby trollers, monitor the colorscope for signs of fish and bait, watch for rips and bottom structure; and somehow get striped bass or bluefish to strike the lures. It's the skipper who keeps the grinders busy. It's the grinders who make the skipper's job look easy.

Equally important is an experienced crew. Trolling should never be boring, even with few fish strikes. A superb mate or knowledgeable crew member should be checking lines for weed, watching rod tips to be sure lures are pulsating just right, scanning for birds, orchestrating the line depths as the bottom rises and falls, and working hand in hand with the skipper. An efficient captain and crew will almost always out-fish the casual fisherman. Remember, luck is being ready for the right opportunity. If you're asleep at the wheel and miss the opportunity, luck will pass you by.

A charter skipper can make wire-line trolling look deceptively simple, while a rank beginner can make it look very difficult. So, let's see how experienced wire liners make it look so easy.

WIRE-LINE TACKLE

Years ago the popular reels for wire line had to have a stainless steel or a hard-chromed spool because Monel and stainless wire could cause extensive corrosion problems between the spool and the line when exposed to saltwater. Traditional wire-line reels never had a levelwind, and gear ratios were only in the range of 2.5:1 to 3.2:1, which is slow by today's standards. All three problems have been largely overcome with new reels from Penn, Daiwa, Okuma and Shimano that rely on modern technology to lick these problems.

Popular classic reels included the Penn 500M Jigmaster, Mariner 49H, Senator 112H and 113H; and the Daiwa Sealine 300HW and 400HW. These were the standard tools of the trade for many years because they had chromed or stainless steel spools. The Penn 112H and 113H are still manufactured today and are very popular with many traditionalist trollers.

With no more care than would be directed at a chrome-spool reel, modern reels with their 4.2:1, or higher, gear ratios, aluminum spools and beefy levelwind mechanisms are proving to be up to the task of wire-line trolling. Dramatically improved anodized finishes that are much less subject to severe corrosion require only a minimum

The Penn 113H is enormously popular as the traditional standard for wire-line trolling, but levelwind reels like the Shimano Tekota are also finding favor because of their powerful gear ratios.

of care to avoid problems. Yes, stainless steel and Monel wire will still corrode an aluminum spool if minimal maintenance and care is not provided, but reels washed with a mild soap solution (the same soap used to clean your boat), then rinsed with a fine spray of freshwater, wiped dry with a soft towel and then spritzed with a spray oil will last for many seasons with absolutely no problems. This is exactly the same care that should be administered to a stainless or chrome-spool reel, so there's no appreciable difference in terms of end-of-trip routine maintenance between the old reels and the new.

The opinion on levelwind reels is changing. Up until recently, only googans used levelwind reels because they were prone to failure under the extreme stress of wire-line fishing. Today's levelwind mechanisms, however, are much beefier and offer several advantages. Wire-line fishing is all about getting the lures to the exact feeding depth of the striped bass. All wire-line trollers use marks on the line to calculate the trolling depth, but additional depth control is achieved by measuring the amount of line released from the spool as the levelwind guide makes one complete left-to-right passage. On the Shimano Tekota 700 this is about 15 feet of line. Knowing this, it is easy to add or subtract increments of 15 feet of line to fine-tune the actual trolling depth.

For instance, with 200 feet of wire in the water, the lure is running at about 20 feet of depth. If a reef comes up to 18 feet, crank in two passes of the level wind and get the lures to rise to 17 feet— just off the top of the reef. This ability to accurately fine-tune the trolling depth gives the angler a lot more control over the lures and the depth they travel.

The levelwind is also of great value to trollers who fish at night because they do not have to keep track of the line when cranking it back onto the reel when fighting a fish or when checking lures for weed. Experienced trollers like to think they have an educated thumb to guide the wire neatly onto the spool, but every veteran also has at least one horrible story about a bad snarl at some time in his career. Severe snarls in wire require that the line be cut from the reel with pliers; not a happy proposition when you've spent a lot of time carefully marking the wire. A sturdy, reliable levelwind mechanism eliminates this problem.

Old-time reels with relatively small-diameter main gears could not provide any appreciable cranking power when the gear ratio exceeded 3:1. The shape of the gear teeth and the overall larger size (diameter) of the pinion and main gears in today's higher speed reels provides cranking power that was not dreamed possible until several years ago. Anyone who has reeled in a fully-armed shad-rigged umbrella knows that cranking in a heavy, water-resistant lure is no fun—you need arms like Popeye and a weak mind to enjoy this part of trolling. This chore becomes much easier with high-speed 4.2:1 gears that take in up to 33 inches of line for every handle revolution; and they do it with the angler barely breaking a sweat.

The higher gear ratio also gets fish to the boat more quickly and has more power to do so. Instead of battling the rod and reel, the fisherman fights the fish, not the tackle. It is essential to keep the line tight when pulling wire line against a big bass. To keep the line taut, many skippers bump the boat in and out of gear to retain some forward motion. This saves fish, but makes it much harder for the angler to reel in the catch. A high-speed reel reduces the need to use the boat gears to keep the line tight and this makes the angler happier. You will hear fewer "Come on, Captain, you're killing me," complaints from your crew if you switch to modern high-speed reels.

SPECIAL RODS FOR WIRE

Because of the abrasiveness of wire, rods must be equipped with AFTCO hardened stainless steel roller guides, tungsten carbide guides, often called carboloy guides, or heavily braced Fuji Silicone Nitride II guides. Standard hard-chromed guides will wear out in a single day of hard fishing, and simply cannot be used for wire-line fishing.

Roller guides work well, but several of the wire-to-leader connections will not fit through the guides. Some traditionalists prefer rollers because the ball-bearing supported rollers significantly reduce friction and make retrieving the wire line so much easier. Because old habits die hard, the most popular guides are still the carboloy type, however, the ultimate wire-line guide is the Fuji Silicone Nitride II. They are the slickest, most durable guides, capable of withstanding the abrasive wire and yet smooth enough to be used with monofilament or braided lines as well.

Opinions on rod actions vary widely. Many anglers like stiff rods when trolling wire especially when they are looking for big fish, yet the best rods are those with a medium action that allows some bending and flexing of the rod while trolling. Since wire has no stretch, a soft rod helps cushion the jolting strike of a big fish, and helps keep a tight line while fighting the fish. Rods of 6 to 7 feet are best with a medium taper to give more action to lures like swimming plugs, jointed tube lures and even umbrella rigs and spoons. The large bunker spoons, so popular off New Jersey and the south shore of Long Island, work best with long, soft rods of about 10 feet in length.

Medium- and soft-action rods have another advantage that helps maintain the action of the lure. As the boat enters a swell or wave while trolling, the boat will tend to slow down momentarily then pick up speed slightly as it leaves the wave sliding into the next one. This speed up, then slow down of the boat can ruin the action of some lures, especially bunker spoons. When trolling with soft-action rods, the blanks, which are bent way back, sweep and pulsate forward as the boat slows down upon entering the wave, keeping the lure working. The rods bend back again as the boat speeds up as it pushes through the wave. The lures, especially bunker spoons, work more consistently with soft-action rods.

Wire-line trolling rods should be equipped with an aluminum gimbal at the butt and have heavy-duty, machined aluminum reel seats for strength and durability. Aluminum Unibutts and so-called hard nylon "slick butts" offer non-stick surfaces that will not get hung up in rod holders when a big fish strikes and is hooked up. A foam butt grip, especially when wet, sticks in the rod holder as if glued in place and can be extremely difficult to remove to fight the fish.

WIRE LINE CHOICES

There are three popular wire-line choices; Monel, stainless steel and braided stainless steel. Monel is a unique copper and nickel alloy that is soft, resilient and heavy. It is less "springy" than stainless and is easier to spool on the reel. It's a little more expensive than stainless steel but since it resists kinking, it tends to last longer than stainless steel. It sinks to a slightly lower level than stainless steel wire.

Yard for yard, stainless steel wire weighs slightly less than Monel so it does not attain the same depth. The difference is so slight that most trollers never even notice. Stainless steel line is much springier than Monel and can be difficult for beginners to handle. It also kinks more easily than Monel so care must be exercised to avoid any twist or kinks that could cause a line breakage. Stainless steel wire is less expensive than Monel.

In Chesapeake Bay many trollers prefer braided stainless steel wire. The line is much more supple than single-strand wire and is a pure delight to work with. It is slowly finding favor with deep trollers further up the coast. Its one drawback is that making connections between the backing and leader is not as easy as with single-strand wire. The connections, however, are made with a small crimp or with an Albright knot and are not terribly difficult. To allow the connections to pass through the guides with no snags or hang ups, add a small length of heat-shrink tubing over the connection.

RIGGING A WIRE-LINE OUTFIT

Rig a wire outfit by first installing the backing, either monofilament or Dacron. Whichever you choose, it should be one pound-test rating heavier than the wire line itself. If you are fishing with 40-pound test wire, the backing should be 50-pound test. Mono is less expensive and easier to handle, but it stretches and eventually deteriorates with exposure to sun and the environment. Dacron is slightly more costly, but has no stretch so it matches the physical attributes of the wire, and it is virtually indestructible. Dacron may get slightly discolored from lying next to the wire line on the spool, but it lasts a long time, does not rot and does not lose strength when exposed to sunlight. Some wire-line fishermen like the Dacron because it has no stretch, an important factor when using wire for jigging bucktails or when fishing for the largest kind of striped bass.

The first time you rig a wire outfit is the most difficult because you will not know exactly how much backing to place on the reel. Too much and the wire won't fit on top of the backing; too little and the spool diameter is too small and the reel is only partially filled, causing a loss of mechanical advantage when cranking in line. If you are an old hand at wire fishing, you probably know from past experience just how much backing is needed, but if you are a newbie you'll need to do some experimenting—but only once. Use a Magic Marker pen and make a reference mark about three-quarters up the side of the spool. Fill the spool with backing to this mark, and then add the wire. Usually the wire will easily fill the rest of the spool, and still leave some space on the reel spool to allow for angler error if the line is not re-wound perfectly while fighting a fish. If the wire won't fit, re-wind the wire back onto the service spool, remove some backing and re-install the wire. Take notes so you can refer to them next season when you replace the old wire. It's better to have the reel slightly under filled, than filled to the very rim edge of the spool. Too much line is a disaster waiting to happen if you get slack in the line and it springs off the spool.

How much wire do you need? Well, this varies depending upon where you fish. Most fishermen use 300 yards of wire, but in the strong rips of Montauk, 350 yards is about right. In Raritan Bay, where some of the best bass trolling takes place in relatively shallow water, a 150-yard shot of wire is all that is needed. If you are not sure, check with a local tackle shop to get some pre-rigging advice.

When making connections between the wire and the backing and between the wire and the leader, a haywire twist is the preferred connection on the wire side. If you are proficient with knot tying, use an Albright to join the backing to the wire, and the wire to the leader. When neatly tied, this connection easily and cleanly travels through rod guides, including roller line guides. There is a problem, however, if the line ever breaks and a new leader must be added to the end of the wire. The Albright knot can be difficult to tie in a bouncing, rocking boat with watery fingers on a bone-chilling day, or in the dark of night.

An easier connection utilizes small barrel swivels, like the SPRO and Sea Striker type, which will pass through the carboloy and aluminum-oxide guides. A simple clinch knot attaches the mono or Dacron backing to one side of the swivel, while the standard haywire twist connects the wire to the swivel. After reeling the wire onto the reel, connect the leader to the wire with the same clinch knot-swivel-haywire twist combination. A large snap swivel is added at the end of the leader with a clinch knot. A 15-foot leader of 50- to 80-pound test is recommended to provide some shock absorption when big fish strike the lure, and also a measure of abrasion protecting if a fish dives under the boat. Add a small plastic bead at the end of the leader before tying on the snap swivel; your rod tip will appreciate the protection.

Some wire liners are now using loop-to-loop connections between the wire and the backing, and the wire and the leader. Instead of a barrel swivel between the backing and wire, a 12-inch loop is formed in the backing with a loop splice (Dacron only), or a Spider hitch or a Bimini twist in the monofilament leader. The backing loop and haywire twist are then looped together making a

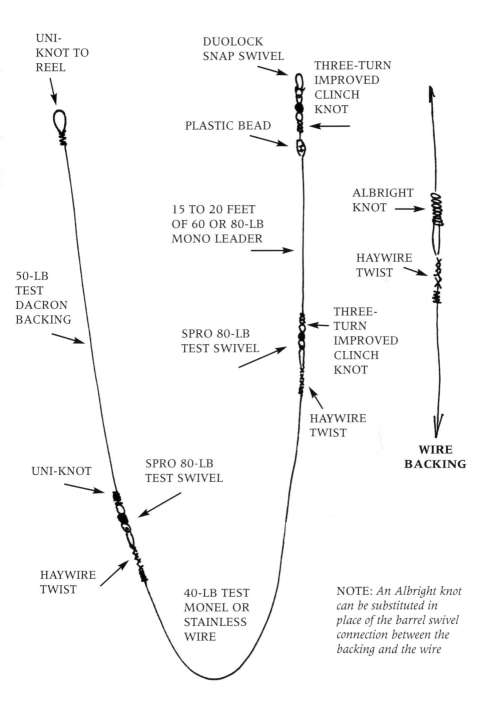

UNI-
KNOT TO
REEL

DUOLOCK
SNAP SWIVEL

THREE-TURN
IMPROVED
CLINCH
KNOT

PLASTIC BEAD

ALBRIGHT
KNOT

15 TO 20 FEET
OF 60 OR 80-LB
MONO LEADER

HAYWIRE
TWIST

50-LB
TEST
DACRON
BACKING

SPRO 80-LB
TEST SWIVEL

THREE-
TURN
IMPROVED
CLINCH
KNOT

HAYWIRE
TWIST

**WIRE
BACKING**

UNI-KNOT

SPRO 80-LB
TEST SWIVEL

HAYWIRE
TWIST

40-LB TEST
MONEL OR
STAINLESS
WIRE

NOTE: *An Albright knot
can be substituted in
place of the barrel swivel
connection between the
backing and the wire*

RIGGING WIRE LINE

neat, small connection that goes through guides very nicely. To make a loop in the leader use a surgeon's knot and then loop-to-loop it to the haywire in the wire. In my experience, the loop connections make a neater connection than the barrel swivel, but the lines can fray at the loop junction causing a line failure in the future. If you use the loop connections, be sure to check the lines and re-tie the connections if any signs of wear are evident.

Charter skippers can't stop fishing if a wire line breaks. Having a back-up rod and reel combo is one way to stay in the game in case of line or equipment failure. Another good insurance policy is based on pre-rigging the wire in 150-foot shots and then connecting them together as needed. Line failures usually occur near the terminal or lure end of the wire where the line may possibly kink while handling fish at boat side, or if the line is not spooled properly while fighting a fish. With pre-rigged 150-foot shots, the damaged shot can be removed and a new length of wire can be added quickly so the boat is immediately back in business.

Some skippers go one step further and connect the two 150-foot shots of wire with a hi-vis Dacron or mono connection. You can accomplish this with the barrel swivel connection, loop-to-loop connection or with an Albright to haywire twist connection. The hi-vis lines are an additional reference mark when calculating depth and allow quick replacement of part of the wire if failure occurs.

CALCULATING THE DEPTH TO FISH

Every boat, every tide, every lure will fish differently while trolling wire, but as a general rule of thumb when trolling at 3 knots you can figure that for every 50 feet of wire you have IN THE WATER, the lure will run 5 feet down. If you put out 150 feet of wire, your lure will run about 15 feet down. Naturally, the action of the lure itself, the speed of the boat, the rate of water current and surface water chop or swells will have an effect on how deep the lures will go.

Mark the wire at 150 feet and then at every 50 feet thereafter. It is unusual to troll with only 50 or 100 feet of wire in the water, so there's no need to mark the wire at less than 150 feet. If you are using separate 150-foot shots of wire, you only need to mark one of the shots at 50 and 100 feet. When connected to the first shot, the second shot marks become references for 200 and 250 feet of total wire. The connection between the two shots becomes the 150-foot reference.

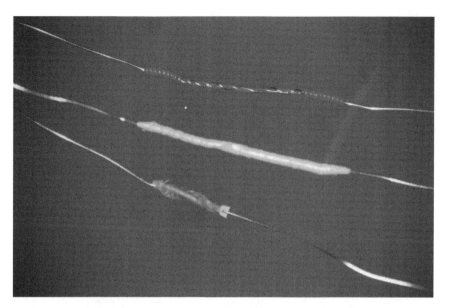

To calculate trolling depth, wire line must be marked at 50- or 100-foot intervals. Telephone wire (top) is the most popular, followed by plastic tape (center) and rigging floss/rubber band combo.

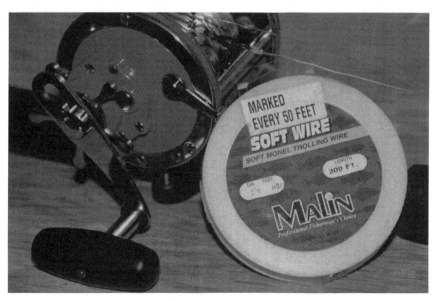

Malin Wire Co. offers Monel and stainless steel wire factory pre-marked at 50-foot intervals, which saves a lot of time when spooling wire line on the reel. The marks are durable and will not move even with hard use.

Marking wire use to be a real chore; not as bad as a sharp stick in the eye but not much better than an hour in the dentist chair. Malin Wire Company changed all that when they began marketing their unique pre-marked Monel and stainless steel wire. The small plastic marks won't move and they relieve the wire liner from having to spend a lot of time stretching out the line on a dock or along the curb at home to apply marks. There is a special place in fisherman's heaven for Ken Ehlers and the crew at Malin; thank you.

If you have to mark wire on your own, there are three methods that have worked very well; telephone wire, plastic tape, or a rubber band and dental floss combination. You need a lot of space to stretch out the wire, such as a dock, along the curb at home or in a local park or ball field, and a tape measure. Yes, your nonfishing neighbors will wonder what you're up to, but most will pass it off with, "There's crazy Joe the fisherman. I feel sorry for his poor wife and kids. Why can't he play golf like the rest of the men on the block?"

The telephone wire method of marking wire is the simplest and most efficient. It uses small-diameter, soft telephone wire intertwined to the main wire to make a mark that is highly visible and doesn't slip or slide along the wire. You can buy the plastic-coated wire at the hardware store or pick up small scraps of it for free at the base of the telephone pole on the nearest street corner. A 6-inch length of colored telephone wire is bent to the wire line so that the wire line and the telephone wire intertwine with each other for about 4 inches. The tag ends are then barrel wrapped to finish off the mark. It is essential that the two wires, the telephone wire and the wire line, intertwine or crisscross one another. The crisscrossing is what holds the wire in place so it doesn't slide.

Wire marks made from 3M elastic tape are another easy alternative. They are inexpensive and require little time. They have one major pitfall. If you don't wrap enough tape on the wire the mark may slide up or down the wire. A moving mark does little to tell you how deep your lines actually are. Lay a 12-inch strip of 1-inch wide tape on a clean plastic cutting board and slit the tape lengthwise into quarter-inch strips. Lay a strip of tape along the wire and make a spiral wrap towards the leader end of the line for about 6 inches, then wrap the tape back over itself toward the reel end of the wire. When finished, the wrap should be neat, small in profile to slip through the guides and it will be immovable. Prior to using pre-marked wire, I used tape wraps for years with no trouble at all, and no slippage. The marks are easy to feel while fishing at night and are easily visible during daylight hours.

Another excellent marking system uses a rubber band and dental floss. To make this system work with little effort, make up a small board with three finishing nails 6 inches apart in a triangular pattern. Stretch a rubber band around the nails, then lay the wire along one leg of the rubber band triangle. Wrap a series of half hitches with the dental floss around the wire and the rubber band. After wrapping for about an inch, cut the floss and the tag ends of the rubber band. When the tension on the band is released, the swelling of the rubber as it returns to its normal unstretched diameter holds the entire mark tightly in place. Apply a coating of Hard As Nails nail polish, then spray paint or use an ink marker to color the mark, and you're ready to fish.

The marks can be color coded for quick reference by using different color telephone wire or 3M tapes, or by applying ink or paint. It's easy to get distracted and forget how many marks you have let out, so using colors can be very helpful, especially when fishing with buddies that may not fish often or be very experienced. Just say, "Let out the line until you see the yellow mark."

Wire is sold in 100-yard lengths and so most fishermen put this amount on their reels. It is also sold in bulk spools with over 1000 yards of wire, which is the way to go if you are rigging two or more wire outfits, or need to install more than the standard 100-yard shot, such as boats trolling off Montauk where strong currents apply pressure against the line and "lift" it higher in the water.

If you need to get the lures deeper than the wire will take them, you can add trolling drails. For every 4 ounce drail you will add another 5 feet of depth. If you want to reach the 40 foot level, let out 300 feet of wire, which will get you down 30 feet (6 lengths of 50 feet), then add 8 ounces of drail for the next 10 feet for a total of 40 feet of depth.

TACKLE AND RIGGING FOR LEAD CORE

Trolling with lead-core line in saltwater is not as popular as it once was, yet some fishermen still prefer it. Lead core has several advantages; it doesn't kink like single-strand wire, doesn't require rods with special guides, it's relatively inexpensive and connections to the backing and leader are easily made. It is also available in a wide range of pound tests from 14 to 60 pounds, making it very versatile for some light-tackle deep trolling.

On the downside, lead core's relatively thick line diameter has a lot of water resistance and when comparing equal pound tests, it takes a bit more lead core to achieve the same lure depth as single-strand Monel or stainless wire when 300 feet of line is let out. When trolling with 100 to 200 feet of lead core the depth results are similar to wire. The more lead core that is let out, the greater the water pressure against the line and the less effective the line becomes. Lead core is usually dyed with varying colors along its length and the colors change every 10 yards. For every ten yards of line in the water, lead core goes down about 3 feet. If you need to reach fish holding at 18 feet, let out six colors of line.

RIGGING LEAD CORE

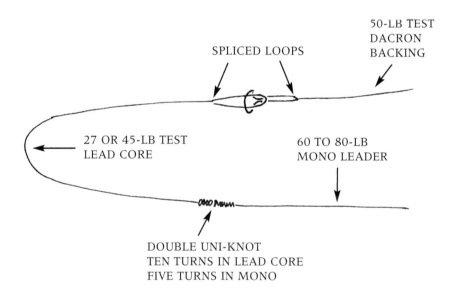

50-LB TEST
DACRON
BACKING

SPLICED LOOPS

27 OR 45-LB TEST
LEAD CORE

60 TO 80-LB
MONO LEADER

DOUBLE UNI-KNOT
TEN TURNS IN LEAD CORE
FIVE TURNS IN MONO

NOTE: *Remove a section of the lead core before making the eye splice to backing or the uni-knot to leader*

The lighter pound tests of lead core can effectively be fished on relatively light conventional tackle. Trolling sandworms along the western shore in Long Island Sound was productive using a 20 yard shot of 18-pound test lead core for school stripers and some trollers use 27-pound lead core in the Cape May Rips. The fun of fishing on relatively light rods and reels is enhanced with the lead core, and in some situations is preferred over wire.

Connections between lead core and the backing are best with a loop-to-loop connection. Remove a 12-inch section of the lead core from its hollow Dacron braided sheath and make a spliced loop, which is then lopped to the loop on the backing. To add a leader, again remove a small section of the lead core, then tie opposing uni-knots to bend the mono leader to the lead core. Make only three turns in the mono, but five or more in the lead core.

BUCKTAIL JIGGING

Jigging a single bucktail on a wire-line outfit is a unique way to get up-close and personal with striped bass. Unlike trolling with the rod in a rod holder, when parachute jigging, you feel the jolt of the strike, and after the fish is hooked, you feel every head shake and tail sweep as the bass makes its runs against the drag. Because jigging is hard work, the rewards when you hook that big pajama fish are that much sweeter and you become part of a select group of bass fishermen who are willing to go the extra mile to catch their favorite fish. This technique is called jigging because of the angler's efforts to sweep the rod thereby make the bucktail dance with an erratic, pulsating action that can drive striped bass into a feeding frenzy.

You can use any wire-line rod between 6 and 7 feet in length, but the best rods are homemade from offshore trolling rod blanks. One of my favorites is a 30-pound class blank of approximately 5½ feet in total length. A fancy version would have a reel seat and foam grips, but mine is simply made with cork-tape handle and the reel is clamped into place. Its short length is ideal for working the jigging action needed to make the lure dance.

To work the jig effectively, the rod is held with the tip pointed at the water, and the butt end pointed toward the sky. If you're right handed, the right hand is held at about shoulder height and grabs the rod at the butt, the left hand is held at about waist level and grabs the rod at the fore grip just ahead of the reel. While facing the stern, and with the rod tip pointed at the water and slightly astern, the angler pushes the right hand away and pulls the left hand in towards the body—much like paddling a canoe. This makes the rod tip sweep forward, momentarily speeding up the lure. Allow the rod tip to slowly drift back so it is again pointing astern. As the wire line comes tight, begin the forward sweep again. Repeat this action until a striped bass hits or your arms become inoperable. That's when it's time to turn the rod over to a buddy and let him get some exercise.

It's most comfortable to jig while standing at the stern corner of the boat's cockpit. Since the rod tip is pointed downward toward the water, a short 5½-foot rod is much more comfortable to fish than a longer 7-foot rod.

A less tiring alternative is to stand next to a wire-trolling rod that is placed in a gunnel rod holder. Face aft so the rod tip is just over your right shoulder. Reach up to the tip top and palm the wire as you slide your gloved hand down to your side. Don't hold the wire, just let it slide across the palm of the glove. By swinging your arm behind you, the bucktail is swiftly accelerated. Allow your arm to relax and drift back towards the stern, pulled by the water resistance against the weight of the bucktail and the wire. When the line comes tight, sweep your arm back again. Repeat and repeat and repeat.

The old-time Smilin' Bill bucktail was a favorite of striped bass trollers many years ago and still catches fish today. Add a strip of Uncle Josh pork rind and you have some striped bass history in your hand—and a great bass lure. As good as the Smilin' Bill is, most any large bucktail will work. Although white is a favorite color for the bucktail head, the pork rind can be white, red, yellow or green for added flash and color.

The so-called parachute jig improves on the standard bucktail design by adding excess hair over the forward, or head, portion of the bucktail. In the water, the forward hair folds back over the bucktail making it pulsate and breathe with a lively action. Pork rind is again added for motion and color.

TIPS WITH WIRE

Wire line has quirks that make it tricky to deal with. First timers using wire often get so discouraged when they experience back-lashes, snarls and kinks that they vow never to use the stuff again.

It also has quirks that make it so easy and efficient to use that it has been steadily employed by charter skippers for a half century. There must be something to this!

Backlashes are probably the single most common problem and they occur whenever the spool begins to spin faster than the line coming off of it. Backlashing is made worse by the wire line's own inherent springiness, and without careful control of the spool, backlashes can be a huge problem.

Wire line can backlash and tangle if thumb pressure is not placed on the spool while paying out line. Many trollers will also leave the reel's clicker button engaged for additional spool resistance.

Thumb pressure on the line is essential to keep the spool from accelerating too quickly. I also recommend leaving the clicker button engaged. The sound may be annoying to some fishermen, but the clicker mechanism applies just enough resistance to prevent the spool from speeding up. When I charter fished it was something I insisted upon. I could listen to the clickers and tell which lines were going out and at what speed. Experienced wire-line trollers will not need to do this, but for newcomers, it's helpful.

Lures with a lot of water resistance, such as umbrella rigs or swimming plugs, take line from the reel with a steady pull as soon as they are streamed in the water. Judicious thumb pressure will handle them well, with no backlashing. Light lures, however, require some help from the angler to pay them out. Since they have such little water resistance, light lures cannot pull the wire from the reel on their own, and if the angler stops applying thumb pressure, thinking that will help the spool turn, the springiness of the wire may cause a snarl, or backlash. Let out light lures with sweeps of the rod tip. With the rod tip pointed aft, sweep the rod tip forward and reduce the thumb pressure on the spool to allow some line to be pulled from the reel. Repeat this process several times until there is sufficient pull from the wire and the lure to allow the natural water pressure to continue to take line from the spool.

Thumb control is also needed to avoid snagging bottom when letting line out. The pressure of the lure and the wire can take line from the spool very quickly; so quickly that the lure essentially dives and goes straight to the bottom before the reel is put into gear to begin trolling. On sandy bottom the worst that can happen is snagged weed or a clamshell, but over a rocky area, the lure could be lost and valuable fishing time wasted. Thumb pressure is required to maintain a steady, but not overly fast, pay out of the line. It can be helpful to stop the spool briefly during line pay out to eliminate any chance of snagging bottom.

Line snarls can occur on reels without a levelwind whenever an angler does not pay attention to careful re-spooling as line is gained while reeling in the fish. If the line builds up too high on side of the spool, then collapses in a pile, the resulting tangle can be fatal. Avoid this by careful guiding of the line with the thumb of the hand holding the rod and reel.

CHAPTER 6

Trolling with Downriggers

No doubt about it, downriggers are the best, most efficient way to plumb the deepest waters for bluefish and striped bass, especially when the depths exceed 50 feet. I've trolled big, alligator-size bluefish in the fall that ran between 14 and 18 pounds in 90 feet of water with the fish hugging the bottom, and what made it all so sweet was the relatively light 15-pound test tackle we used to pull bright green tube lures. Those hefty blues were very sporty to catch, put up a terrific fight and tested the angling skills of the crew.

Downriggers can also be used to fish near the surface of the water. That's one of their most significant advantages; the ability to present lures anywhere in the water column from 10 to 120 feet below the surface. The angler has complete control to present the lures at any depth from shallow to deep and with the ability to fine-tune the trolling depth to keep lures in the feeding zone. As an example, New Jersey's Shrewsbury Rocks is famous for good striped bass fishing, but the rocky bottom rises and falls dramatically, and many a rig, spoon or plug has been lost to these rocks. In particular, one of the best spots is a sharp rise to 18 feet that is a consistent producer of striped bass, but it's also a very "hungry" pinnacle that eats lures like kids eat candy bars. With downriggers, it's a simple task to raise the weight, skim the top of the structure and hopefully hook the biggest bass of the day. A skillful captain and crew can quickly raise and lower the trolling weight to instantaneously adjust to any structure profile when fish are hugging the bottom. The skipper watches the fishfinder and lets the crew know to crank in or let out the downrigger lines.

Downriggers also offer enhanced maneuverability while trolling. Unlike braid and wire, which usually require up to 300 or more feet of line in the water to achieve their trolling depth, downriggers need only stream 50 to 100 feet of line behind the trolling weight. The shorter line allows the skipper to make the boat dance like a ballerina, and making sharp turns to maneuver through a crowded fishing area or to spin the boat to get back on a good piece of structure is a breeze.

The fight with the fish is much more pleasant and enjoyable with downriggers since the fish is battled on a relatively short line. You can also use lighter tackle if you wish to increase the sport of the day's fishing. A long length of mono stretches like a rubber band and dulls the fight of the fish by cushioning the pulling of the fish against the rod and reel. A long length of wire or lead core is heavy and requires a strong back to reel in the fish. Because of the relatively short line, downrigger-caught fish are much more exciting to catch.

My first experience with downriggers was back in the late 1970s. The results in terms of fish caught were very encouraging, but the equipment did not hold up very well in the salty environment. Early downriggers were designed for sweetwater salmon and lake trout fishing, and could not handle the corrosion problems that are normal for coastal saltwater fishing. That quickly changed, however, and downriggers of today are constructed of corrosion resistant aluminum, stainless steel, and super-tough space-age plastics that are quite capable of dealing with a life in the saltwater world. My pair of Penn Fathom-Masters are now over 25 years old and are still in excellent shape, requiring only minimal maintenance, and I expect they will continue to provide many more years of reliable service.

Downriggers are not inexpensive, ranging in cost from just over $150 for a basic manually operated model to over $1200 for electric models with a long list of built-in features; but based on their years of service, the cost per year is minimal. A well-equipped mid-priced downrigger will set you back about $250, about the same price as a good rod and reel outfit. A friend of mine has been using a pair of manual Cannon downriggers for 17 years and figures it only cost him about $13 per year. He also caught his 51-pound striped bass on a downrigger; and that's priceless.

DOWNRIGGER CHOICES

The basic downrigger has a large-diameter spool to hold the trolling cable, a crank to reel in the cable, a line counter to track how much cable is deployed, a clutch system to release the line, a boom to keep the line and the trolling weight away from the boat, a trolling weight to take the lure down to the depths and a release system to let go of the line and lure after a fish strikes and is hooked up.

Upgraded downriggers add on features like electric motors to do the paying out and retrieving of the cable, and additional automatic functions so the angler can pre-program trolling depths and stop the trolling weights just below the surface on the retrieve.

The length of the boom that is best for your boat depends upon where you will position the downrigger while fishing, and whether the boat is inboard or outboard powered. For an inboard boat, most trollers like a short boom that angles directly off the stern. This places the downrigger trolling weight and line release clip within easy reach of the angler or mate without leaning too far over the side. On an outboard boat, some fishermen will still use a short boom, but prefer to angle the boom at 90 degrees from the side of the boat. Again, it's within handy reach and the weight will not bounce into the side of the hull. Some trollers prefer a longer boom and use a swivel base to swing the

Downriggers are a time-tested trolling method for catching trophy stripers and jumbo bluefish, and can be adapted to any boat, large or small.

boom and weight toward the boat to gain access to the trolling weight and line release clip. This system works well, but care must be exercised so the swinging boom arm does not allow the weight to crash into the side of the boat, or into the transom.

Some downrigger models offer telescoping booms that can be adjusted to suit the best length for your particular boat. This handy feature is so popular it is often the determining factor when deciding which downrigger to purchase.

Another popular accessory is a rod holder mounted directly onto the downrigger, and another is a flush-mount rod holder adaptor. Many inboard or big-boat saltwater boat owners do not want to ruin their cover boards, especially if they are teak finished, by drilling holes and installing permanent downrigger mounting pads. I mount my downriggers on quick-mount adaptors that slip into a standard rod holder so I can quickly add the downrigger, and just as quickly stow it when not in use, and leave behind no visible (spelled u-g-l-y) mount pads on the boat. Small-boat owners may not mind the standard screw-in mounting pads, and if they are installed close to the transom they can be positioned to be unobtrusive, yet still handy to use.

Adding an accessory rod holder directly to the downrigger allows for more efficient deployment of the tackle by keeping the rod and reel close to the rigger and uses fewer of your flush-mount rod holders. These adaptors are very sturdy and can withstand firmly set drags and big fish. To be sure the downrigger and tackle are secure to the boat, add a safety line for each downrigger and another line for the rod and reel.

Some downrigger manufacturers make trolling weight storage simple by installing a handy hook at the base of the outrigger boom. While cruising from one fishing location to another, the trolling weight is attached to the hook on the boom and is thereby prevented from swinging wildly. If your outrigger does not have a hook, it is a simple matter to purchase a 2-inch long, ¼-inch diameter threaded stainless steel bolt, with an eye hook on the end, at any marine supply store and do the job yourself. Leaving the weight hang off the end of the boom while cruising at speed will quickly wear out the end of the trolling cable and probably cost you a lost weight.

The weights can also be stored on the deck while cruising. Place a wet towel under the weight so it doesn't scratch the deck, and be sure the cable is slack so it doesn't cut across the edge of the cover boards and scratch the fiberglass or gel coat.

Downrigger trolling weights come in many styles and shapes, and each manufacturer has its own design that it believes is the best for most fishing conditions, including cannon ball, cannon ball and tail fin, torpedo shape and wing shape. There are also after-market trolling weights with a built-in diving wing, fish silhouettes and actions that set up fish-attracting vibrations. Weights range from 4 to 15 pounds. For saltwater use, the heavier weights are generally a better choice.

Some weights have a natural lead finish with no color, while others are coated with special epoxy or poly paints in colors that extend from red, white and chartreuse to bright orange. There are two schools of thought; one says the colored trolling weights attract strikes, others feel the bright colors spook the fish. In deep water, most colors disappear, so the argument becomes moot, but in shallow water, color may play a part in your success, or lack of it. I've been quite happy with standard uncolored lead trolling weights, but I've met too many good bass trollers that swear the colors help. Like the guy in the arcade says, "Hey, you pays your money, you makes your choice."

Two styles of line clips are available; pinchers that grab and hold onto the line, and line clips that trap the line in a wire bail or a roller. The grabber type will work with saltwater lures that do not have a lot of pull in the water such as single tubes, small spoons, small swimming plugs and bucktails. For lures with a substantial pull, such as bunker spoons, umbrella rigs and swimmers with large swim lips, the wire or roller type releases are better choices because they have much higher tension settings. I've been using the Black's and DuBro bail releases and the AFTCO Roller Troller, which is my favorite. The roller assures absolutely no line wear from chafing or fraying, and the screw adjustment for the release setting can be cranked down to provide enough tension to even hold a fully armed shad rig.

When fishing very light lures or lures with minimal water resistance, the pincher-type release is a good choice because it holds the line firmly in place and the line cannot move. Once you set the drop back, it stays until a fish strikes the lure and pulls the line from the clip. With a roller or bail-type release, excess water pressure on the fishing line that runs from the rod tip to the trolling weight and

Lures with a lot of water resistance, such as shad rigs and umbrella rigs, can be fished off downriggers with an AFTCO Roller Troller line release clip. The clip can be adjusted to hold any lure, light to heavy, and is essential to trolling success with downriggers.

release clip can exceed the resistance of the water drag on the lure. The water pressure on the line running between the rod tip and the trolling weight causes the line to billow away from the boat and is called blow back. If water pressure on the blow-back portion of the line exceeds the water resistance of the lure, the line between the lure and the weight will be pulled through the roller clip toward the trolling weight until it is riding up against the weight. This is not good. To overcome this, when using a bail or roller-type line clip with light lures, a rubber band can be twisted around the line, and then attached to the clip.

One of the most successful striped bass trolling lures is an umbrella rig armed with a full compliment of plastic shads. The ulti-mate hotshot colors along my part of the coast are chartreuse and pearl. Trolling these lures on wire line or a super braid with an 8-ounce weight was previously the only two ways to get them down deep. If you didn't like wire-line fishing, or if you didn't like streaming 300 feet of braid, you were out of options. The AFTCO downrigger release clip changed all that. Captain Chuck Salkeld showed me how he twisted the adjustment nut until the AFTCO clip would stay shut, even under the extreme pressure of a shad rig, until a striped bass whacked the lure. Once free of the line clip, the angler could fight the fish on 100 feet of line and have a great time with the fish.

Some fishermen have expressed concern that the cable running from the downrigger down to the trolling weight can cause a hum or vibration that spooks fish. While I have not experienced this problem, if cable hum is a problem for you, try using one of the braided downrigger lines. I've used the PowerPro downrigger braided line with excellent results. This is a special braid manufactured specifically to replace downrigger cables. Its diameter is smaller than the standard cable and cuts the water cleanly so the trolling ball or weight runs deeper with less cable (braided line) in the water.

TACKLE RECOMMENDATIONS

Downriggers can be used with a wide range of tackle. I've done some stunt fishing with 8-pound test light spinning gear to catch teen-size blues on the troll; yet when I charter fished, I went to the other extreme and used 30-pound gear because on a good day it was not unusual to catch well over a hundred bluefish in a few hours, or jumbo fall stripers that often exceeded 30 pounds. For the private boat, 20-pound gear is about right.

Most of the tackle covered in the chapters on trolling with mono and super-braid lines applies to fishing with downriggers. In fact another excellent advantage of fishing with a downrigger is the ability to use the same gear as you would employ for other types of fishing, such as jigging, bottom fishing or casting. Getting dual use from a pair of rods and reels helps defray the cost of the downriggers.

While it's true you can get double duty from some tackle, you will also be a more efficient downrigger troller with a rod and reel dedicated to the downriggers (or an identical pair of rods and reels if you fish two downriggers). An example of an all-round outfit is the Penn International 975CSLD filled with 30-pound fine diameter monofilament or 50-pound braid and matched to a Lamiglas BL7030W or St. Croix SWC66MH. This outfit can handle a wide range of fishing situations with plenty of line capacity if you hang

Most downriggers can be outfitted with an optional quick-mount adaptor that slips into a standard rod holder. An add-on rod holder mounted on the downrigger keeps the rod and reel within easy reach of the angler and crew.

a trophy fish. It's typical of the exact same rod and reel rod selection that might already be in your tackle arsenal for other types of fishing. There are many alternative rod and reel combinations from Daiwa, Shimano, Quantum and Okuma from which to choose.

A holdover from freshwater trolling is the belief that a long rod with a soft tip is essential. I have not found this to be the case, and in the salt chuck the opposite is probably true. The rod should not have the action of a pool cue, but neither should it be so flimsy in the tip, as are the freshwater rods, that it loses all ability to fight a decent-size fish. With all due respect to our freshwater brethren, there's no comparing a salmon with a big bluefish or a 30-pound striped bass. To successfully fight saltwater fish, a rod with a powerful butt is mandatory. I've tried several of the salmon-type rods and found them to be much too weak to be effective. A good saltwater downrigger rod must combine a powerful butt action with a sensitive tip that can be flexed with a good bend when the rod is loaded while trolling. Standard rod lengths of 6½ or 7 feet are ideal.

Up until recently, spinning gear was not generally recommended for serious trolling when bigger fish are the target. This has changed in the past several years with the increased popularity of braided super lines, and with the advent of spinning reels with significantly improved gear and drag systems. Ten years ago, it was a rare spinning reel that could dish out sufficient drag to set the hook while trolling; unless the fish were small schoolie-size bass or so-called cocktail blues of only a few pounds. Many spinning reels can now reliably maintain a drag setting of up to 15 or more pounds, which is quite sufficient to set the hook, then play a decent-size fish. A 15-pound drag setting would be ideal for 30- to 50-pound test line, which is identical to what would be used with conventional trolling gear.

I've tried several spinning reels from Fin-Nor, Okuma, Shimano, Penn, Quantum and others that worked just fine when trolling with downriggers. While most serious trollers looking for trophy catches would still opt for conventional tackle with its inherent superior mechanical advantage when fighting fish, spinning is still a solid choice when you want to dial in an extra measure of challenge and sport when battling gamefish on light tackle.

SETTING OUT THE LURES

Using a downrigger for the first time, it may seem like you need a crew of fourteen to hold the tackle, clip the line to the weight, lower the ball and steer the boat. Experienced downrigger trollers have developed and fine-tuned their techniques so that deployment of the gear is simple, takes only a few seconds and can be done by one person!

There are many variations that will work for you, but here's how I do it in my Parker center console—by myself—and it is essentially the same sequence I used for many years in larger inboard boats, and it works with spinning and conventional tackle. To start, the downrigger trolling weight should be at the end of the boom and ready for use, and the line release clip pre-set to hold the line without tripping until a fish strikes. I'm assuming the downrigger has an accessory rod holder attached to it. I know that I usually stream 100 feet of line, so I pre-mark my fishing line with an ink marker or a dozen twists of rigging floss or a rubber band as a reference. The reel's drag has been pre-set to one-third the breaking strength of the line and the reel's clicker button is set to the On position.

Get the boat headed in a straight direction. With the reel in free spool, hold the rod and reel in the right hand with the thumb on the spool. Place the lure into the water and begin to pay out the line until about 25 feet of line is in the water. Apply thumb pressure to stop the spool, and move the left hand to the rod tip to grasp the line and hold it firmly. With the left hand holding the line so no additional line will stream out, place the rod and reel into the rod holder on the downrigger. Use both hands to reach out to the downrigger weight and attach the line to the release clip. Let go of the line and simultaneously lower the trolling weight. Place the fingers of the right hand on the reel spool to apply slight tension to avoid a backlash and smoothly pay out line from the reel. When the trolling weight reaches the proper depth, tighten the downrigger spool control to stop the cable. When the 100-foot mark on the line passes through the tiptop guide, engage the reel into gear. You're ready to troll and it probably took just as long to read this sequence as it does to actually let out the line—only a few seconds.

At the strike of a bluefish or striped bass, the line clip releases the line and the angler can now fight the fish unencumbered by the heavy trolling weight. It's a good idea to reel the trolling weight to the surface. If you are fishing with two or more downriggers, you'll have to decide whether to haul in the other lines and downrigger weights. The size of the fish is usually apparent immediately after the strike. If it's a standard-size bluefish or a small to medium striped bass, I leave the other lines in the water in hopes of a second hook up, or to be ready to make another pass over that same spot as quickly as possible. Medium-size fish can usually be controlled with a minimum of boat handling, but I will raise the trolling weights to a mid-depth range, still keeping the lures in the water while the fish is played. Only over very rocky and relatively shallow water will I take in the other lines. While playing the fish, the boat is typically bumped into and out of gear to maintain position in the wind and sea, and this is enough to keep the lines streaming tangle free.

CALCULATING THE DEPTH

Water pressure will apply force against the downrigger cable so the trolling weight is not directly beneath the boat. The angle of the cable can be in the range of 15 to 30 degrees, and so you need to let out a bit more cable than the depth you wish to troll. As a rule of thumb, I let out about 25 percent more cable than the depth I want to reach. For instance, if the fish are marked at 50 feet, I let out to 60 feet of cable. Since bluefish and striped bass will rise to attack baitfish, even if I'm not exactly at their feeding depth, strikes are still assured. If the angle of the cable to the trolling weight exceeds 45 degrees, you need to slow the boat.

TROLLING WITH A DOWNRIGGER

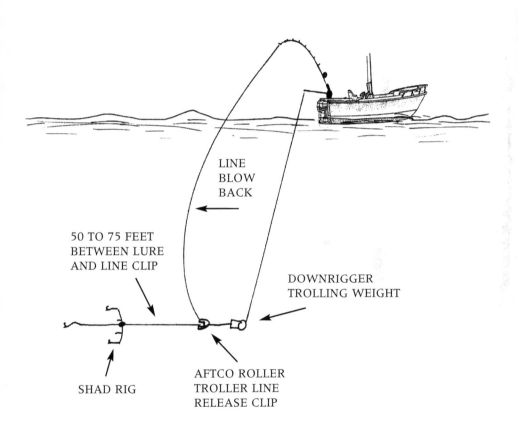

LINE
BLOW
BACK

50 TO 75 FEET
BETWEEN LURE
AND LINE CLIP

DOWNRIGGER
TROLLING WEIGHT

SHAD RIG

AFTCO ROLLER
TROLLER LINE
RELEASE CLIP

Many years ago when I first tried fishing with a downrigger, I thought I had hit the mother lode of bluefish. As I approached an inshore ridge, I set out the lines and immediately began marking a lot of fish, but after several passes over the ridge without a hit, I assumed the trolling weights were not deep enough, so I let out more cable. The "fish" marks on the fishfinder moved lower. Hmmmmm, what was going on? I let out more cable and the "fish" marks again went lower. I cranked in several yards of cable and when the "fish" marks moved higher, the light bulb went off—I was marking the downrigger weights, not fish! That particular fishfinder had a wide cone angle and could read objects and fish at quite some distance from the boat. It was an experience for a good chuckle, but more important, it helped me learn exactly how deep my lures were running. It showed me that I needed about 25 percent additional cable. It took about 38 feet of downrigger cable to get the trolling weight to 30 feet of depth.

MIX 'EM UP

The ability to troll a third line off a downrigger while at the same time trolling with two wire, mono or braid outfits is another unique advantage, especially in small boats where trolling three wire-line outfits, even with outrodders to help spread the lines, can be a difficult challenge. Too quick a turn or a hook-up with a fish that runs over one of the other lines can both cause unbelievable line tangles. Since all the lures are traveling at approximately the same depth and the same distance from the boat it's easy to figure out why this occurs—too many lures in too small an area.

Adding a third, even a fourth line, into the pattern with a downrigger can be accomplished with virtually no chance of a tangle because the downrigger line is fished much closer to the boat. Let's say we have a pair of wire outfits pulling bunker spoons at 30 feet of depth on 300 feet of line. A third line fished off a downrigger would also be positioned at 30 feet of depth, but with only 100 feet of line streamed in the water. The downrigger lure and the wire line lures are 200 feet apart and the chance of a "honeymoon" tangle is remote.

The most significant problem in mixing trolling lines is the opportunity for multiple hook-ups. On a large boat with a four- to six-man crew, the task is relatively easy to overcome, but on a small boat with only two anglers, a three-fish hook-up is quite challenging—but a heck of a lot of fun!

CHAPTER 7

Trolling Strategies

It pays to get on the trolling grounds early. The magic hour at sunup is often a great time for striped bass.

Many striper fishermen would rather catch their fish while casting or jigging; but truth be told, most stripers will be taken on the troll. Spring blues are scattered and not yet settled into tight, compact schools and trolling is the best way to score a good catch. In spring and fall, trolling is the grunt work required to catch good numbers of bass or bluefish on a day-in, day-out basis. It's a technique that charter skippers rely upon, and which small-boat anglers can use to score some big-time catches, too. Even if you plan to jig the fish after you have located them, trolling is still the ideal way to search good structure to find the fish.

Placing your lures directly into the dining room of Mr. Bass or Mr. Blue is critical if you want to score with consistent success, and as we've seen in previous chapters, there are several ways to accomplish this; monofilament, wire line, lead core, super braid or downriggers.

The technique you choose will be decided by your own preference for which technique you enjoy fishing the most, tempered by the unbiased information provided by the fishfinder. The fishfinder should be your ultimate guide when deciding which trolling method is best on any given day. As we begin this discussion on trolling strategies, let's review the strong points of each trolling method.

The time-tested mono and mono-and-drail trolling methods work well in waters no deeper than 20 feet, or when fish are located near the surface. A 4-ounce drail and a ponytail lure will work just fine for bluefish holding in the top 10 feet of the water, while an 8-ounce drail and a shad rig with a 2- to 4-ounce center weight will reach down 10 to 15 feet of water depth, which is well within range of stripers holding on a shoal, sandy lump or sandbar. Trolling with a mono and drail combo also works well when trolling along the surf line just outside the breakers, and in shoal areas along many coastal beaches at dawn when striped bass and bluefish will begin moving from the shallow surf to their deeper daytime holding areas some distance off the beach.

Single-strand wire and lead core is the favorite choice when fishing in 20 to 40 feet of depth. Wire takes the lure down 5 feet for every 50 feet of line in the water and is the traditional choice for most striped bass and bluefish trollers from Massachusetts to New Jersey. Add a 4 or 8-ounce drail, and you'll get another 5 to 10 feet.

Super-braid lines are appealing to a wider audience of striped bass and bluefish trollers because they are so easy to use. With an ultra-thin line diameter, 50-pound super braid slices through water like 12-pound test monofilament. A shad rig with an 8-ounce drail will go down about 25 feet—just perfect for many of the same areas where wire line is usually employed. The beauty of using super braid is in the tackle. A typical light inshore trolling or jigging rod can be employed and the entire outfit is much lighter in physical weight, and more pleasant to use.

Downriggers are the best way to plumb the deeper waters. Areas within the 3-mile EEZ that exceed 40 feet are prime candidates for downrigger fishing for striped bass. Bluefish, of course, can be caught anywhere you find them, and some of the distant inshore structure in depths of 60 to 120 feet can be effectively fished.

There is some overlap. For instance, shallow water can be trolled with monofilament, braid or a downrigger. When fish are located in mid-depth ranges braid, wire and lead core, and downriggers can all be used, but when the fish are very deep, the only choice is a downrigger.

QUICK MATH REVIEW

Accurately calculating the trolling depth is critical to success. With Malin's pre-marked wire, the calculations are easy; 50 feet of line in the water gets the lure down 5 feet. For super braid, use a Magic Marker every 100 feet, or tie in an 80-pound size 6 SPRO barrel swivel every 100 feet. When using a 4-ounce shad rig, for every 100 feet of super braid in the water, you'll reach about 7 feet of depth. Add an 8-ounce drail to get an additional 10 feet of depth.

When fishing downriggers, the scope of the trolling wire away from the boat must be taken into account. Veteran downrigger trollers add 25 percent to the trolling depth to make up for this scope. If the striped bass are marked at 25 feet, let out 30 feet of downrigger cable.

SETTING UP THE BOAT

Large or small, the boat must be set up for efficient trolling operations. The crew must have quick, easy access to the tackle, gaff or net, spare lures, pliers, fish gloves and other accessory gear. The deck should be uncluttered and the rod holders positioned so the angler and mate can get at them without struggling.

Outrodders are must-use equipment for mono, braid, wire and lead core, and are essential to productive trolling. Safety lines should always be used to make sure the outrodders and the rods and reels stay in the boat. For no-budge security, I wrap and tie the outrodder safety lines under the gunnels to the bottom of the flush mount rod holder. One safety line is for the outrodder, another is for the rod and reel.

Catching big bluefish on the troll, like this one caught off Oregon Inlet, requires teamwork between the angler and crew.

Place a rubber mat or a wet towel under the cooler/ fish box so it doesn't slide around the deck, and have it about half full of ice, either block or cubes so it's ready to chill the fish you catch. I like to add two or three gallons of seawater to make a super-cold slush that keeps the fish cold as possible and very fresh.

To be ready for every fishing opportunity, stow extra lures where they can be accessed quickly, but still stowed out of the way so the crew is not stumbling over them while they walk the deck to let out lines, play fish and do the usual chores of trolling. A cabin boat has the advantage of keeping lures dry and accessible in Rubbermaid or Tupperware boxes, mesh storage pouches or in 5-gallon buckets. Center console boats have less dry storage, but can still store extra lures and tackle forward of the console, or inside the console. Striped bass trollers are very inventive when it comes to thinking up great ways to store their tackle. Regardless of where and how you elect to store your gear, a primary consideration should always be to keep the deck clear, but the tackle ready for quick access.

A typical day of trolling wouldn't be "normal" if a tackle problem or two didn't jump out and bite you on the butt. Line or knot failure, a jerky drag, a jammed free-spool mechanism, a broken guide—from big to little, problems occur and having back-up tackle ready is the best way to meet them head-on and with a quick solution. Whenever the Murphy's Law, "Whatever can go wrong, will go wrong," rears its ugly head, having a spare rod and reel, pre-rigged and ready is the best solution. If nothing goes wrong during the day, hey, that just makes the fishing trip so much sweeter; but don't be lulled into complacency because you'll owe one to Murphy on the next trip.

With today's minimum size and reduced bag limits, if you score a great day of bass fishing, you will have to release many fish. To do so you'll need a net and it must be stowed for quick, tangle-free access. The tangle-free part can be a challenge; nets seem to grab every protruding reel handle and hook, and can even get wrapped around rod tips. Many boats have a rocket launcher system of rod holders at the aft end of the boat's hard top, and stowing a net there seems logical; until the net swings in the breeze and gets wrapped around a spare rod and reel. When you need it most, you'll waste essential time trying to untangle the net. A short bungee cord or heavy-duty rubber band like the type sold in commercial fish supply stores wrapped around the net bag so it holds the bag close to the net handle can be a big help and reduce your need for aspirin.

Lay out leadering gloves, pliers for hook removal and fish tags at the helm, on top of the cooler lid or on a bench seat so these items are within handy reach of every crewmember. If you fish with different friends on most every trip, take a few minutes before leaving the dock to explain to everyone where all this stuff is located and why it's needed so they can help you work the cockpit efficiently and boat the fish quickly.

As you head away from the launch ramp or your dock, there is usually a few minutes of idle time while cruising to the inlet or the open water where you'll be fishing. This is a great time to check the tackle, check and set the drags, be sure the clickers work, the rod guides are all okay, the leader isn't frayed and that the lures are on deck and ready to be clipped to the snaps. If you have newbie anglers on board, take a minute to explain how the reels operate. It's a good idea to explain what they have to do and what they can expect to happen. These few minutes can save a lot of heartache and frayed nerves later.

FINDING FISH

Okay, we're out past the breakwater, throttles shoved forward and we're on our way, but where will we start trolling? Actually the decision should have been partially made the day prior to the trip by checking with your buddies and local tackle shop to get the latest skinny on where the hot bite has been. Remember that even negative news is potentially "good" news because knowing the areas that weren't productive yesterday saves you time today by eliminating those spots that probably don't have fish today.

After reviewing the verbal reports you collected, it's essential to check the logbook and hot spot list. The day's trolling plan should combine the on-the-dock information with a plan to troll over the most productive structure in the areas where fish were most recently caught. For instance, if I heard that striped bass action had been good at the clam beds off Island Beach yesterday, that information is helpful to narrow down where I will look today; but I will review my logbook and jot down the Lat Lon locations of other nearby structure such as the deep hole off the pier, the 60-foot rough bottom, the shoals off the Governor's House, and other areas that have produced fish for me in past years. By hitting all these areas, chances are very good that striped bass will be found and a few fish will be slipped into the box for dinner.

To be consistently successful, a good troller must be aware of changing weather and sea conditions, bait movement, bottom structure and temperature breaks.

If no info was available from the previous day, such as might happen after several days of windy weather when no other boats got out, then the logbook information becomes even more important. It identifies specific places where fish were caught in the past under similar conditions and so it offers the best guidance on where to go today. Striped bass and bluefish are both creatures of migrational habits and rhythms, and where you found them last year at this same time, is very likely where you will find them this year.

There are several variables that also require consideration, such as wind direction, sea surface temperatures, current, sea conditions and ambient light.

Steady winds of the same direction can move fish from one location to another. For striped bass this movement may only be a few hundred yards or a mile or two, but for bluefish, wind can move the fish many miles from one day to the next. Bluefish traveling north in spring may move more quickly with a south wind, but hold steady with a north wind. Striped bass often hold close to the beach when the winds blow onshore and hold the bait in the shallows, but the bass move away from the beach after two or more days of steady offshore winds push the bait to deeper water.

Wind can also influence water temperatures. While a southern wind is often thought of as warming wind, this is only true for land temperatures. A southwest wind can move warm surface water in an offshore direction, allowing the cooler lower layer of water to rise. The cooler surface water can move fish long distances as they try to maintain their position in the warmer water.

Sea and weather conditions also have to be factored into today's trolling plan. If yesterday's weather had choppy seas, stiff winds and cloudy skies, and the bite lasted from dawn to noon through an entire tide period, the same fishing should occur today if the same conditions occur. If they change, however, to sunny skies and calm winds, the good bite may only occur at first light through dawn and stop as the sky gets bright.

STRUCTURE EQUALS FISH

Striped bass and bluefish are not found willy-nilly widely spread out over the ocean. They travel along specific and predictable routes that correspond to structure edges. Structure can be changes in the bottom, rip lines where two currents rub or along the edge of a temperature change.

Of the three types, bottom structure is the most significant and holds the most potential to locate gamefish. What is bottom structure? It's any significant change in the bottom such as a ridge, hill, slope, slough, channel edge, steep drop-off, a drop-off along a beach or a sharp rise. In shallow water a change of only a foot or two can be enough to hold bait and gamefish, while in deep water the change usually has to be more significant. Along shore, any point of land that juts out toward deep water is always a good place to look for striped bass and bluefish.

Rips will form where two currents rub against one another, usually at an angle, or in opposing directions. Rips may also be formed as current washes over a relatively shallow bottom structure such as a shoal, sand bar or around a point of land. Gamefish will hold in or near the rip to feed on bait that washes toward them. Rips formed over bottom structure have their fastest current at the top of the rise, so gamefish will lie just in front of, or just behind the rip. Where two currents rub, the fish could be on either side of the rip so it pays to try both sides.

Temperature breaks may also combine with rips formed by currents, such as outside an inlet where the warmer water from a bay washes out to the cooler water of the ocean. The water between Montauk and Watch Hill is a huge "inlet" releasing and taking back huge amounts of water from Long Island Sound. Similar rips and temperature breaks occur in Raritan Bay, Delaware Bay and Chesapeake Bay. Then there are the dozens of inlets that empty from creeks, rivers and back-bay waters all along the coast. In spring the warmer water will usually hold the fish, but in the heat of summer, the bass will look for cooler water.

When trolling for bluefish, look for bottom structure, offshore rips formed by an upwelling of current, offshore weed lines, temperature changes and water color changes. Each of these opportunities can hold promise of excellent fishing, but only the bottom structure will be predictable day after day. Currents, weed lines, temperature breaks and color changes are constantly evolving and change frequently, but bottom structure is always there. The skillful troller looks for the changing opportunities and takes advantage of them when found, but only bottom structure can be relied upon to give up fish on a steady basis.

SETTING OUT THE LINES

Big crew or small, setting out the lines requires everyone's cooperation, and some common sense seamanship. If the boat is headed on a straight course, two lines can be streamed out simultaneously, but it is essential that the boat's course remain straight and true. Any turning at this point will bring the lines closer together and a tangle could result. If one line is already in the water, a tangle is easily avoided by making a slight turn so the line being streamed is on the outside of the turning radius. The line that is already in the water will be pulled along the inside curve of the turn and will remain out of the way of the new line.

While paying out the lines, maintain thumb pressure on the spool to avoid a backlash and to prevent a heavy lure from plummeting too deeply where it might snag on bottom structure. A well-coordinated crew can get the lines in the water more quickly if the skipper momentarily increases the boat speed by kicking up the engine rpms slightly.

Working the lines and handling the fish takes a coordinated effort to maximize the fishing potential, and to avoid tangles and problems. An experienced crew makes it look easy.

Once the lines are at their correct distances, reels are engaged into gear, clickers set to the On position, the rod and reels placed into outrodders or downrigger rod holders, and safety lines are attached.

Once the lines are streamed out and the actual trolling begins, the crew should watch the rod tips for proof that the lures are working correctly. The actions of the lures pulsate up the line and the rod tips do a rhythmic dance when everything is working just right. Any time the dance changes; it could mean weed or a snag of some other floating material. Shad rigs transmit minimal action up the line, so watch the bend of the rod. Any increase in the rod's bent arc will indicate weed. To avoid tangles, any time you have to reel in a lure to check for weed, make a shallow turn away from the line being reeled in so it is on the outside of the curve.

TROLLING TECHNIQUES

Presentation is everything. The lures must be presented to the fish at just the right depth and speed for maximum success as a troller. The "wrong" color or size lure will occasionally catch if it's presented at the feeding level of the fish, while the "right" lure will catch nothing if it's way too high above the fish, way too low, or way too fast or slow.

The depth of the fish is determined by the fishfinder. It allows you to peer through the surface and becomes your eyes to "see" what is below. It shows bottom structure and the feeding depth of the fish. Depending upon the feeding depth, make your choice of mono, wire or downrigger, and then adjust the trolling speed.

Bluefish are more aggressive and may strike at most anything you troll past them, but striped bass will not be fooled by a poorly presented lure. The lure must look real and act naturally in your opinion, but don't forget that your opinion doesn't always count. With a brain the size of a pea, striped bass and bluefish are not Einsteins, however, they aren't stupid either. They have street smarts that trigger a warning bell when a trolled lure looks phony. The lure must have realistic action, travel at the right speed and be presented in the right direction.

Action and speed are inter-related. A fast, whirling tube lure traveling at 4 knots is a killer for bluefish, but gets no action from stripers. That same lure traveling at 2¾ knots will be ignored by bluefish, slammed by stripers. Your GPS will display the trolling speed of the boat. If you are marking bass and blues on your scope, and only catching bluefish, you are trolling too fast. Get the engine rpms down and try a slower speed to score with the bass.

Depending on local currents, the GPS display of the boat speed can be accurate, or badly in error. In areas with little current flow, the GPS display will be right on the money, but a strong current will alter the action of the lure. Trolling against a 2-knot current with a boat speed (Course Over Ground) of 2 knots will make the lure swim as if it were actually traveling at 4 knots, which could be okay for bluefish but too fast for stripers. Trolling with a 2-knot current at 3 knots boat speed actually makes the lure swim as if it's traveling at 1 knot, which minimizes the lure's action and gets no strikes. Trolling against the current requires a slower boat speed to compensate for the speed of the water flowing past the lure, while trolling with the current requires a faster boat speed.

A striking fish will give away some much-needed information for the skipper. For instance, when making a turn, the angle of the lines from the lures to the boat changes and the two trolled lures tend to come closer together. For this reason, sharp turns are to be avoided, especially when trolling with wire line, lead core or braid. While making the turn, the outside lure will rise slightly higher as the outside line speeds up slightly. The inside lure slows slightly and runs slightly deeper. A strike on the outside lure tells you that the fish are responding to a faster trolling speed or that the lure should be trolled higher in the water. A strike on the inside line is signaling the need to slow down or run the lures slightly deeper.

The trolling direction can be very important. Whenever there is a significant current, bass and blues will usually face into that current, and they'll wait for baitfish to come tumbling to them. In areas of strong current the bait will never swim into the current past a waiting striper. The bait will hold in a safe area where there is little current in order to save energy. A trolled lure coming from behind a striper may spook the fish and move it off the structure. Whenever there is a strong current, try trolling sideways to the current.

There is no hard and fast rule for the "best" trolling speed, but as a general rule of thumb most striped bass prefer a slower lure speed, bluefish prefer faster lures. There is some overlap with school stripers that will often hit lures trolled at bluefish speeds; but for those big cow bass, slow is better. Typical big-bass trolling speeds run from 2 to 3 knots, while bluefish speeds will range from 3 to 5 knots. To maintain a very slow striped bass speed most twin-engine boats must troll with only one engine in gear, and if your boat can't get slower than 3 knots, try towing a 5-gallon bucket on a short rope to slow the boat.

Some striped bass sharpies use a prop with less pitch so that at idle the prop digs less water and therefore allows a slower trolling speed. If you try this, be aware that at slow- to mid-range engine rpms there's no problem, but don't run at wide open throttle or the engine can be over-revved and damage could occur.

TROLLING IN THREES

Presenting three lures in the trolling pattern can dramatically improve the overall catching power of the lure spread, however, the potential for lure tangles also increases, especially if sharp turns are required, as is often the case when trolling in areas where numerous other boats are plying the same bottom structure.

Adding more lines to the trolling pattern can help you catch more fish. With wire lines set out to the sides in outrodders, one or two downriggers can be added at the transom corners. If done correctly, the wire-line lures and downrigger lures will be about 100 feet apart, but at the same trolling depth.

The tangles occur when the three lures are all fished at the same depth with lines of equal length. By presenting the center lure at a deeper depth and on a shorter line, tangles become much less of a problem. This can be accomplished in two ways; use a downrigger for the center lure, or fish the center wire line rod with an 8-ounce drail ahead of the lure.

The wire lines will usually be streamed about 200 to 300 feet behind the boat and with the rods in outrodders to achieve as much side-to-side spread or separation between the lures as is possible. With only 100 feet of line in the water, the downrigger line is separated at a substantial distance from the two wire lines because it is much closer to the stern of the boat.

If the third rod is equipped with a wire line, an 8-ounce drail added to the leader will require about 100 less feet of wire to reach the same depth as the two wire lines fished to the sides of the pattern, which again effectively keeps the center lure separated from the two side lures and away from possible tangles.

With a beam of 8 to 9½ feet, three rods is about maximum for most outboard boats; but wide-beam boats, especially big inboards boasting a beam of 12 to 15 feet, trolling with four rods is possible. When trolling with four rods, the most effective pattern usually employs two downriggers, one at each stern corner; and two wire rods, one to each side mounted in outrodder holders.

TAKE NOTES AND KICK BUTT

I keep a pencil handy at the helm while trolling so I can make notes directly on the gel coat surface at the helm (it wipes off), or in a small spiral notebook. Small things can make a big difference in your success and I write them down to be sure I don't misinterpret or forget them.

You will encounter days when the fish will only strike the lures when trolled in one direction; write it down. This could be due to currents, angle of the sun or wind and sea conditions, which cause slight differences in trolling speed. Write down the colors of lures that are catching the fish. If one particular umbrella rig with all-red tubes is the hero, write it down. Or maybe it's a green hoochie, purple deep diver, chartreuse and white bunker spoon—whatever it is, write it down.

Write down things that might be helpful later in the day. "Bait at the point," or, "Bass on south side of the channel at marker 12." Even if you get no strikes now, the fish may bite like mad dogs later in the day or at the turn of the tide, and writing down notes about locations of bait and fish concentrations can be just the thing you need to save a slow day.

Mark which way the boat was headed when you get a strike. After going back over the same spot a few times, and if you get more hook-ups, a pattern becomes obvious indicating in which direction the fish want to strike the lures. For instance, when trolling over a reef with a mild current, if the first three fish were all caught while trolling in a southerly direction, then you can eliminate wasted time by trolling over that reef only in a southerly direction. At the next hook-up, as you play the fish, boat it, then reset the lines; make a wide turn that takes the boat back to the north to begin another southerly set. Good striper skippers often work these long circles to get into position for a good pass, in the right direction, over a small piece of structure.

If you mark fish that are deeper than the range of your wire, you can add a 4- to 8-ounce trolling drail to gain an additional 5 to 10 feet of depth. You can also take the boat out of gear for a brief few moments, which lets the lures sink deeper, and then shift back into gear and begin trolling again. The lures will drop to a deeper level, then surge upward through the school of fish, hopefully getting a strike.

When fishing a new piece of bottom structure, especially a large one, it pays to work a back and forth trolling pattern that takes the boat over all of the structure. A very small lump may be approached with only two or three passes, but a large piece of bottom real estate will require several, or many, passes to cover it all. If you're working in a north/south direction and mark fish but get no strikes, try a few passes in an east/west direction. The change of direction may offer a more realistic lure presentation.

When trolling along a beach where the bottom drops off into deeper water, the bluefish and striped bass will usually be found cruising along the edge where most of the bait will also take up residence. A trolling pattern that takes the lures across the edge in a zag-zag pattern from shallow to deep and back to shallow again will usually be the most productive approach. On some days, especially when the weather is overcast, the fish may be on the high side of the edge, while on a sunny day, the fish may move to deeper water. It is typical to find bass at a 15- to 20-foot drop-off at first light, but an hour later they will be at the 30- to 40-foot drop-off as the sun rises and penetrates deeper into the water.

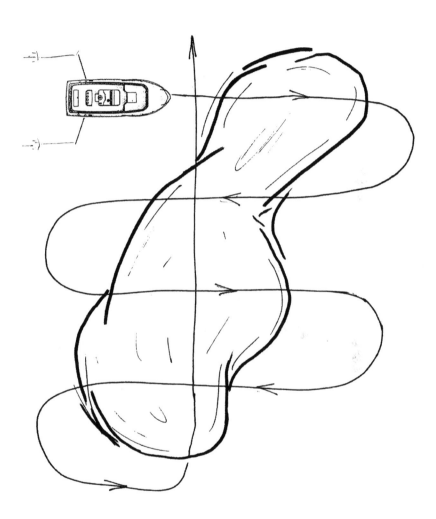

CRISS-CROSS TROLLING PATTERN

If you are marking fish, but getting no strikes, you can also try slower or faster boat speeds to make the lures swim differently. Sometimes it takes a change of only 50 rpms to make the lures more attractive so the fish can't resist striking.

SHALLOW-WATER TECHNIQUES

The overall strategy for shallow back-bay trolling is much the same as for deep water. Find the structure; find the fish. Look for channel edges, shoals, sand bars, points of land, deep holes and creek openings. Take notes and monitor the tackle and lures carefully to gain additional data needed to help make the best decisions.

One old-time technique that has been nearly forgotten is trolling with sandworms on a very simple rig with a Colorado spinner blade or a Cape Cod spinner placed ahead of a 2/0 bait holder hook. A sandworm is draped on the hook and the rig is slow trolled along sedge banks, rocky bottoms, creek mouths, bridges and channel edges with remarkable success. Some sharpies are now using a Berkley Gulp! Sandworm placed on the hook first followed by the real worm placed on the hook behind the fake.

Shallow-water trolling is a great way to locate gamefish. This striped bass was caught on a bucktail trolled along the edge of a marsh sedge.

Shallow-water lures are often just scaled down versions of their big cousins such as plastic lipped swimmers, bucktails, spoons and soft-plastic shads. To enhance the sport, many trollers will tuck the rod and reel under their arm, but if you are spending a lot of time trolling, outrodders are a good idea.

PUT YOUR ELECTRONICS TO WORK

A chartplotter is essential and will definitely help you catch more fish. Large boat or small, bay or offshore, a chartplotter is valuable fishing equipment. Once I installed my first GPS plotter I have habitually used the Save button to track and remember hundreds of good striped bass and bluefish trolling hot spots.

A chartplotter will not only display a chart of where you are located, along with bottom contours and channel markers, but it also plots, or tracks, your boat's progress with a track line as it travels from place to place. It will show you where you've been trolling, where the fish have been hitting and the route you traveled to and from the inlet. A chartplotter can be a big help to every fisherman/boater.

From the moment you leave the dock, start saving locations, especially in places not familiar to you. If you trailered your boat to a new fishing area, when running toward the inlet you may have to navigate a winding, twisting channel. Hit the Save button as you pass markers and buoys, shallow channel edges, fish traps and other obstructions. If you come back later in a fog or bad weather, you will have an easier time navigating back to the ramp.

During your run out to the grounds there are many situations that merit a hit on the Save button; bait location, temperature changes, bottom structure or even a location where someone else is fishing. These are all good things to remember.

You should adjust the length of time the track line remains on the screen. A longer time will also allow you to navigate safely back to the ramp, and while trolling, the track line shows exactly where you've been and the bottom structure you've covered.

When a fish strikes a trolled lure, the first thing to do is hit Save. After the fish is boated, re-set the lines and immediately make a pass directly back to where you hooked up. That saved location probably holds many more fish. At the hook-up of every fish, you should be thinking of catching the next fish. While concentrating on boating the first fish, your mind must be analyzing data and helping you get prepared for bass number two.

On the next pass over that structure, if you don't get a strike right away, keep working the area and make several more passes near and around the saved location. If I'm fishing an area that is not very crowded, I use a figure-eight trolling pattern that takes the boat directly over the exact location of the first hook-up, but which also allows me to take advantage of some carefully controlled roaming with the boat. When I get another bite, I hit the Save button again. After three or more fish a pattern will develop that tells you the direction the fish are moving, and you can then concentrate on making more passes in that direction.

As you keep getting more hook-ups, the accumulating Save marks will give you a good prediction of where the next hook-up may be. This works well when working schools of bluefish that can be seen on the surface feeding and crashing bait, then diving. They are moving quickly and keep popping up in different locations. By watching the progression of the Save marks, you can predict the direction the fish are moving and anticipate where they will be found next. Like the cavalry in an old horse opera movie you can "Head 'em off at the pass."

CHAPTER 8

The End Game

Okay, you're hooked up, now what?

The dance the angler, crew and captain play while fighting a big striped bass is a thrill to watch when an experienced team does the work, or it can be a side splitting Three Stooges comedy when a clumsy crew tries to do the job. Along the journey to success, every good troller has played a part in an embarrassing comedy routine, probably more than once; but this is all part of the game. The learning curve can only go up as you figure out how to deal with problems such as pulled hooks, tangled lines, slack lines, angler error and just plain ol' bad luck.

Every mistake, however, is an opportunity to gain knowledge and to improve your trolling end game. No famous charter skipper or local sharpie ever got to his vaulted position overnight, and everyone who is successful today certainly got there by making plenty of mistakes in the past. How you deal with your share of mishaps, screwups, tackle problems, rough seas, clueless anglers and bad luck, determines your ultimate level of success.

As you make the journey from newbie to sharpie, it's essential to maintain a sense of humor because it's a sure bet the fish will win once in awhile, especially big stripers, and when they do, have the grace and good temperament to say, "Thanks for the memory. See you next time."

Charter skippers have an advantage because they fish with the same mate every day working together as a well-oiled team. Private boats have the same advantage if they routinely fish with the same group of buddies because everyone knows the drill, knows their job and knows what to expect from each other. If you regularly fish with different anglers and crew on every trip you are definitely at a disadvantage, but it's not insurmountable if you spend a few moments at the dock to explain the tackle, safety procedures and the basic trolling strategy. Once on the fishing grounds have someone hold the wheel while you show the crew how to set out lines, how to handle the tackle, and how to set the rods in the holders. Take a moment to explain what has to be done when a fish strikes, how to work the tackle, clear the decks and boat the fish. Your brief rundown will not replace the experience that comes from actually catching a few fish, but at least it gives a new crew some idea of what is expected of them, and what they can expect the fish to do.

At the start of the day with a new crew, use the old "There's weed on the line" excuse to ask one of the new crew to reel in the line and check the lure, then set it out again. Okay, it's a fib, but the act of reeling in the line, handling the tackle and re-setting the lure in the trolling pattern gave the new guy a feel for what's going on and he'll react better when he's really hooked up tight to a decent fish. Besides, you should be checking lines regularly for weed or debris.

Be sure to check and properly set the drag on each reel. At the strike, it may seem like line is literally pouring from the reel. Fishermen and outdoor writers exaggerate with prose that describes "line melting from the reel" and back at the dock nearly every fisherman finds it hard to resist embellishing their stories of a good fishing day and how "that big fish nearly spooled me." In reality, though, a striped bass would find it impossible to empty the spool of a reel holding 350 to 450 yards of line—if the drag is set right.

The only way a striped bass can spool a reel is if the drag is too loose or if a truly huge fish hits on very light tackle. A bluefish or striped bass is capable of running only just so far against a properly set drag. If the reel is set with the drag calibrated about one-third the breaking strength of the line, the fish will simply run out of gas before it takes all the line; and when it stops running, it's time to start grunting and regaining line. It's an eye-opening experiment to set the drag with an accurate hand scale. You will be probably be surprised to discover that what you thought was a tight, firm drag was actually much less.

Let's take a look at some strategies that minimize problems and make it easy for the crew and skipper to look like veterans.

HOOKED-UP

When the rod bends over hard and the cry "Fish on!" announces a hook-up, there's an adrenaline rush that is the ultimate thrill of trolling. Yep, battling the fish is great, but the hook-up is that brief electric moment of jubilation before the hard work begins. Experienced crews savor that moment, but keep their cool and react carefully and deliberately.

What the captain does after the strike and hook-up can be just as important as finding the fish and getting the right lure to them. On a slow day, it's especially tough to lose what might be the only trophy catch, or possibly the only catch, of the day. The best trolling fishermen will use the boat, the wind and current to their advantage. Once the fish is hooked, teamwork from the crew and angler, careful boat handling by the captain and quick use of a pencil are essential to play the fish quickly and to get back to the school of fish quickly.

The angler must keep a bend in the rod at all times, even while pumping a fish, to avoid pulling the hook. After the hook-up, the captain should maneuver the boat to keep the stern to the wind whenever possible.

The captain must keep the boat in gear and immediately press the Save button of the GPS, and make mental notes about the hook-up; which lure, what color, trolling direction, boat speed, was the strike on a turn or straight run, lure depth. A quick pencil entry is made in the spiral notebook kept at the helm. Every GPS plotter has a Save button, but in the excitement and commotion of the strike, it's too easy to think the Save button was pressed, but when we go to call the numbers up, they aren't there. It's impossible to miss with a pencil and a scratch pad, and the numbers can be saved forever. The pencil is often better than the computer. If you don't keep a notebook, scribble the hook-up position on the helm—it will wash off later when you clean up.

The boat is kept in gear for only a few moments (a short five-count will do) in hopes that fish number two will strike another lure. Striped bass and bluefish usually gather in schools, loosely or in tight packs. As the trolled lures cross over the edge of some structure or big pod of bait, there may be several fish that give the lures the look-see. The most aggressive fish will strike and get hooked. His buddies, seeing the commotion, get their competitive juices flowing and get ready to strike also. They'll be hooked in a moment if the boat is kept in gear, they won't be hooked if the throttle is dumped and the engine taken out of gear. Out of gear, the lures that didn't get bit by the first fish will slow down and nearly stop, losing their life-like action. Keeping the boat in gear maintains the lure speed for a few seconds, which is just enough time for one or two fish to strike other lures.

Several things happen all at once after the fish is hooked. As the captain throttles back to idle speed, he leaves one engine in gear to maintain a slight forward motion to the boat. As the boat slows to a crawl, the angler takes the "fish on" rod out of the rod holder and concentrates on keeping a tight line. It's important that the angler wait until the boat is out of gear before trying to lift the rod from the rod holder. Even relatively small fish can exert a tremendous amount of pull when the rod is bent over double and removing the rod and reel without losing your footing on a slippery deck or losing it overboard can be challenging—that's why a safety line is always used.

The angler must keep the line tight by maintaining a bend in the rod and cranking the reel when decreasing rod pressure indicates slacking of the line. If the reel has the clicker in the On position, slide the button to disengage it. Many wire-line trollers may wish to use a gimbal belt to avoid bruises, but more importantly to allow maximum rod pressure to be applied against the fish. If a second rod went over, a second angler attends to that rod in the same manner as the first angler.

Getting the wind off the stern is helpful, especially for small boats and small crews. Fishing in my center console, I often fish alone for striped bass on many mornings, and trying to fight a fish, gain line, steer the boat and reel in the rod and reel that wasn't hit can be interesting; and sometimes quite tricky when plowing into a head sea. Slow the boat too much and a precious lure can get hung on the rocks, maybe losing line and lure. Maintain too much speed and the fish you are fighting can escape by pulling so hard it breaks free.

On calm days center console boats are fun. On rough days when simply standing is a victory, trying to fight a big bass pulling for all it's worth can be nearly impossible for the angler. It's helpful in these rough seas to keep the stern to the fish so the angler can get support by leaning against a rocket launcher, cooler, or gunnels.

When angler, crew and captain perform as a team, big striped bass can be the reward, like this trophy bass caught on a bunker spoon.

As the battle continues, the skipper makes adjustments to the boat's direction as may be needed to avoid other boats, or to help land the fish. Depending on the direction of the wind and the location of nearby boats, the captain may have to veer the boat to the right or left. It's tough to fight a fish with the boat heading directly into or quartering into the seas and wind. A slow turn to the lee will get the wind off the beam, then off the stern where there's less chance of tangled lines. The wind helps keep the lines tight and the fish directly off the stern. The veering turn should be very shallow, not sharp to cause lines to cross or excess line to be lost from the reel.

The crew should be sure the decks are cleared, downrigger weight(s) reeled to the surface and that safety lines are out from under the angler's feet. Leadering gloves are placed on the hands of the wire man, and gaff or net are readied and placed in position for quick access.

As early as possible in the fight, the angler should let the crew and skipper know whether he's hooked into a schoolie or a big mule. School fish require less effort to reel in and unless the seas are excessively rough or if the area is extremely crowded with other boats, the remaining line(s) can usually be left in the water. The skipper should be bumping the boat in and out of gear to maintain a tight line to the fish and to maintain rudder control and steerage of the boat. This is especially important with wire and braided lines that have no stretch. Even the slightest amount of slack in the line may allow a fish to throw the lure, so minimal forward motion is essential to help prevent lost fish. With a small fish on the line, an experienced crew will leave the remaining line(s) in the water, but will often reel the line partway in to avoid snagging on the bottom. With a downrigger, the trolling weight is raised to a mid-depth range.

If a big fish is hooked, the requirement for more cooperation between captain, crew and angler increases dramatically. All lines that did not get a hook-up are reeled in and the tackle is stowed so as not to interfere with the work being done in the cockpit. This gives the captain much more freedom to maneuver the boat with no chance of tangling the hooked fish with another line. The angler is also free to walk the deck as needed to always face directly toward the fish.

Inexperienced trollers often complain when the captain maintains some headway with the boat by alternating in and out of gear.

To the uninitiated, this seems to make the battle with the fish so much more difficult and tiring, but maintaining some slight forward motion after the hook-up saves many fish. Wire-line trollers looking for bass and blues can't allow any slack in the line.

Because they have virtually no stretch, wire line and super braid-line require an extra measure of skill from the angler in order to keep the line tight. It is possible to pump the fish in by lifting the rod tip then lowering it while cranking the reel handle to gain line; but this can only be done in a careful, deliberate manner that never allows any slack line or the rod to lose its bend.

The slightest slack can mean goodbye fish.

This is much less of a problem with monofilament. Because it has so much stretch, this line is very forgiving of angler mistakes until the fish gets nearer to the boat. The shorter the amount of mono between the boat and the fish, the less of a safety factor from line stretch is available.

As the fish gets close to the boat, the skipper should use the engine to keep the boat moving forward slowly. This places the fish right alongside the boat within gaffing range.

Wire, braid or mono, the captain must always keep slight forward motion. It's heartbreaking to be on a trophy bass for many minutes only to lose the fish at boat side because the captain took the boat out of gear. Slight forward motion assures a tight line and can be maintained by bumping the boat in and out of gear every few seconds. We're not looking for speed, just a small amount of forward motion. On twin engine boats, alternating between port and starboard engines keeps the headway in a straight line. As the fish makes a move to either side, simply using the engines can steer the boat to keep the fish off the stern.

BOATSIDE TACTICS

As the angler gains line and the fish approaches the boat, the need for teamwork is more critical when you get eye to eye with a great gamefish. Let me tell you a true story about "the big one that got away" aboard a friend's boat many years ago. It's a lesson I never forgot.

After a strong fight, a big striped bass lay only a few feet away from the boat, inches beneath the water, dorsal fin just barely creasing the surface. I had a good hold of the leader and the Danny plug was solidly hooked in the striper's jaw. The fish should have been ours.

The boat's owner, Jim, took the boat out of gear to grab the gaff. This trophy was going on his wall. As the boat's momentum slowed, then stopped, I had to keep pulling in more leader to keep a tight line to the fish. I ran out of leader as my hand came within inches of the plug and its deadly treble hooks. There was no way I could keep a tight line.

"Get the boat in gear," I shouted to Jim but he was already walking to the transom corner, gaff in hand, where I was leaning over the gunnel looking at the playful eye of the big bass. Do fish sense moments of weakness in anglers? This one must have. It rolled slowly on its side, angled its head away and before Jim could reach the fish with the business end of the gaff, the bass dodged under the boat. I pulled back on the leader trying to turn its head away from the engine but 30-pound line is no match for a 50-pound fish.

The leader rubbed against the outboard's lower unit and I felt it vibrate in my hands for a brief instant before parting. The bass, the plug, the trophy for the wall and the dozens of stories that could have been told as it graced Jimmy's den disappeared in a heartbeat. The great fish was gone. Later that night while re-living the tale with a few friends over a late dinner, Jim admitted, "I should have kept the boat moving. The wind blew us right back over the fish. It was a goner the moment I left the throttle to get the gaff. You can bet I'll never do that again."

This lost trophy illustrates an important point about bringing big fish into the boat; the boat must have some slight forward speed as a fish is about to be gaffed or netted. The forward motion keeps the line and leader tight. Many fish will swim towards the boat as a mate or buddy places firm pressure on the line or leader while maneuvering the fish to the boat. With no forward motion to the boat, the leader man can quickly run out of leader real quick, before the mate is ready to gaff the fish. The result is a lost fish as it spits the hook from slack line or as it rolls under the boat.

On my boat, the engine is put into gear at idle rpms just as the leader is within reach. This forward motion usually causes the fish to rise to the surface and lay on its side or belly, parallel to the direction of the boat. Ideally the leader man should move to either transom corner. Usually the fish makes this decision as it favors one direction as it swims in protest near the transom. A bluefish is less of a problem than a big striped bass, unless you have more than one blue on at the same time. A few hand-over-hand pulls with the leader and the fish should be lying in perfect position for the gaff man to lean over the corner and do his job, neatly and cleanly.

When netting striped bass for release, the angler can lift the rod tip and move a few steps away from the transom to help lead the fish toward the waiting net.

If you are netting the fish, the net is lowered about halfway into the water and the fish is lead into the net at the same time the mate slips the net under the fish. When lifting a big fish in the net, hold the net handle vertical so the weight of the fish is in the bag, not along the handle shaft, which could bend under a heavy load.

Up until the moment the fish is gaffed or netted, the captain applies only enough motion to keep the line tight. Too much speed can cause the fish to be pulled from the leader man's grasp. Usually, I bump the engine shift control in and out of gear several times, applying only enough forward motion to keep slight headway. If a big bass makes a hard turn away from the boat, the leader man releases the leader and the angler again plays the fish. Since the boat is moving away from the fish, if it turns, the fish can't get cut off on props or underwater gear like rudders or struts. As the fish turns, the boat moves away and the fish dodges into the wake, not under the boat.

Since so many striped bass are released these days, good gaffing techniques are becoming a lost art. Assuming all went well and the gaff man has a clear shot, the gaff should be placed into the head area so no meat is destroyed and to get a firm bite into muscle and bone, not soft flesh that may tear and cause a lost fish. At the instant the gaff is struck home, the angler should back off the drag and place the rod in a holder, and the skipper takes the boat out of gear.

The best place to lift the fish is at the transom corner, which is the only clear spot for outboards, stern drives and bracket drives. Even inboards with their clean transoms usually have the lowest freeboard at the transom corners so the lifting distance from water to cover board is minimized. If firmly hooked, fish of 5 to 15 pounds can be hauled aboard by grabbing the leader and swinging the fish over the cover boards. Bigger fish require a net or a gaff.

A special word about handling umbrella rigs and shad rigs is appropriate, especially when dealing with bluefish and small- to medium-size bass of less than 15 pounds. These multi-armed lures can easily snag clothing or flesh if not handled safely. To avoid problems when boating fish that have been hooked on the center leader of the rig, I run my right hand down the line to get a firm grip on the center weight of the umbrella rig. With an extended right arm, I keep the rig toward my right side, keeping it away from my body while sliding my left hand down the center leader toward the fish to grab the lure at the end of this leader. The fish can now be swung aboard and dropped on the deck where it can be safely handled. When dealing with multiple hook-ups, modify this procedure to keep the fish apart and minimize the wild flip-flopping of hooked fish. Big fish can only be handled by gaff or large net.

It takes teamwork to boat a fish and the game plan is the same whether it's a 12-pound bluefish or a 40-pound striped bass.

INVITATION TO DINNER

Fresh fish for dinner is a great reward for all the hard work you put into a tough, long day of trolling. To guarantee the best possible quality of the meat the fish must be carefully prepped for the cooler. Cuts are made to the throat latch and the tail so the fish bleeds out quickly, a process that can be messy, but which is necessary for the finest quality of the fillets. Many fishermen rarely take this simple action, and yet it is essential if you want fish with the mildest flavor.

The reputation the bluefish lug around about their strong flavor is partly due to the lack of proper care by the angler. Yes, big jumbo blues have a stronger flavor than those delicious 2 to 4 pounders, but all blues are much better tasting table fare when bled immediately. Striped bass also develop a stronger flavor, even when chilled, if they have not been bled, a process that only takes a few minutes and delivers the freshest meat possible.

A saltwater brine made from shaved or block ice will provide temperatures that approach freezing. Use Kosher salt mixed with seawater, and chop the blocks into smaller chunks. The fish will be so cold your fingers will hurt as you filet the fish back at the dock, but the fillets will be firm, translucent in color and completely odorless.

It's helpful to have a fish box that can take your catch so it's laid out flat and not bent like a pretzel, which only makes cleaning and filleting a bit tougher.

Excess fillets offer a tasty opportunity for future dining pleasure if stored in airtight bags. A great investment is a vacuum bag food processor to seal the fillets with all the air removed from the bags so there's no chance of freezer burn. My wife, Linda, and I enjoy fish fillets all through the winter because we took the time to carefully package the fillets.

Release your catch carefully and give the fish time to revive if the battle has been lengthy. This striped bass is ready for release and will hopefully spawn in the coming spring.

RELEASE FOR TOMORROW

Striped bass regulations severely limit the number and size of striped bass recreational anglers are allowed to keep for the table, and in many states the striper is blessed with game-fish status. I have one beef with today's regulations because the management-mandated minimum sizes are relatively high, which forces anglers to continually kill fish from tomorrow's valuable breeding stock.

Opinions about striped bass regulations and management schemes are a dime a dozen, and often stir up contentious arguments. I'm probably a lone voice in the wilderness, but here's my two cents; I'd rather see a slot limit for fish of around 16 to 24 inches because these are the best, most tender and succulent fish for the table; and a punch card for a limited number of bigger fish per season. Save the breeders!

Since I fish for fun these days, not for charter, I release virtually all the bass I catch, only keeping the rare fish that gets gut hooked and is bleeding. Having been fortunate to participate in some amazing catches during the 60s and 70s, it was heart rending to see the stocks plummet to near destruction and I'm elated to have the chance to fish again in this revived fishery. The stripers we have today are a gift, bought and paid for by severe sacrifices from commercial and recreational fishermen, and I urge everyone to limit their take of big striped bass. Catch 'em, hold 'em up for a quick photo and then let 'em go. It will make you feel good.

Same goes for bluefish. Those spring 5 pounders are excellent table fare when bled and immediately iced down, but those big 15-pound alligators are better off spawning for another year or two instead of fertilizing the tomatoes. Bluefish are one of the finest gamefish and they deserve your respect.

Tagging part of your catch helps scientists learn more about the migrations, growth rates, population dynamics and relative abundance of striped bass and bluefish, so join the American Littoral Society, Sandy Hook, Highlands, NJ 07732. Pam Carlson will fill you in on how to become a tagger.

The maze of federal and state regulations, plus attacks upon sport fishing by extreme environmentalists, is cause for alarm. We need hard-working people in Washington and at the state level to argue the case for a strong, healthy recreational industry. Without good representation, sport fishing as we know it will end. Charter boats and tackle shops will go out of business, and the freedom to fish that you take for granted will come to an end.

Join the Recreational Fishing Alliance, PO Box 308, New Gretna, NJ 08224; and the International Game Fish Association, 300 Gulf Stream Way, Dania Beach, FL 33004. These two organizations need your support; and you need them to represent you. Please join.

CHAPTER 9

Essential Knots for Trolling

Experienced striped bass and bluefish trollers have learned to rely on a limited number of time-tested knots to attach lures, terminal tackle, leaders and backing, so let's take a look at the most-often used knots, what they are best used for and how to tie them. Fancy-wrapped custom rods, precision reels and a tricked out fishing machine are of little value if the knot in the line which joins the lure and the tackle is inherently weak or poorly tied.

The right knot, properly tied, is the most vital connection between the fisherman and the fish. Even the very best knots cause a slight weakening of the line; the wrong knot, or a poorly tied knot, can cause a major loss of line strength. The choice of which knot to use is an important decision every fisherman makes when tying on a snap swivel or a lure, or when joining two lines together, or when adding a shock leader at the end of the main fishing line.

The goal is to use knots that are easy to tie and which retain as much of the original line strength as possible. These same knots should hold firmly without slipping or unraveling, and they should be quick and simple to tie. Over 200 knots have been developed over the years to fit fishermen's needs, but most of us that troll the edge of the ocean can get along with the following selection of basic knots which can be used to tie a wide variety of rigs.

It is a good idea to tie as much as you can at home at the bench in your workshop. You get the neatest, strongest knots possible in this controlled environment. A blustery day on the water with cold, slippery hands is not the time to tie good knots. In an emergency, yes, but workshop knots are always best.

TEN TIPS FOR STRONG TROLLING KNOTS

1. Neat is good. Twists or spirals should be uniform so when the knot is snug there are no loose coils.

2. Wet the knot with saliva before tightening so the coils come together smoothly.

3. Pull knots tight with steady, even pressure. Jerking the knot causes an intense build-up of heat that weakens the line.

4. Use a glove when tying super-braid knots to avoid cutting your hands when pulling the knot tight.

5. Test every knot. Pull hard after each knot is tied. It's better to have it break now than on a big fish while fishing.

6. Don't be stingy. Use enough line to make the loops and twists easily, with a few inches left over.

7. When tying knots in double lines keep the lines parallel and avoid any twists.

8. Use a small scissors, fingernail clipper or pliers designed especially to cut mono and braid lines. Do not use the same tool to cut wire line. Dedicate a special pair of cutting pliers for wire line.

9. During a day's fishing, check the line frequently for rough spots or frays, and replace as needed.

10. Practice. Knot tying is a skill that is learned only through practice. Try knot tying at your home workbench to become familiar with new knots.

IMPROVED CLINCH KNOT

The improved clinch is preferred by most fishermen when attaching a lure, snap, snap swivel or barrel swivel to the end of the main line or leader. It is easy to tie, very strong, reliable and tests have shown the improved clinch knot provides up to 98 percent of the un-knotted breaking strength of the line depending on how carefully it is tied.

Adding the last tuck of the tag end of the line under the loop formed when the tag end is brought back towards the snap swivel eye is essential for maximum strength. The extra tuck is what makes the knot "improved" over the old clinch knot and it prevents the knot from slipping, which is the main reason for knot failure. Leave out the extra tuck and the knot loses about 25 percent of its strength.

When tying the improved clinch knot in a heavy leader, such as 60-pound mono or fluorocarbon, it may be impossible to get five coils to draw up tightly. In this case use only three or four turns, not five. Although fewer turns are not as strong as five, the leader is still far stronger than the main fishing line.

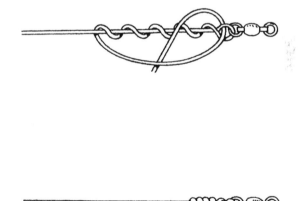

For added strength, the double improved clinch knot is often used, especially for lines under 20-pound test. Fold about 24 to 30 inches of the line back on itself, and then tie the knot with the two strands of line in exactly the same manner as if they were one strand.

At the start of each new fishing day, it's a good idea to re-tie any improved clinch knot that is used to attach a snap, snap swivel or swivel to the end of the main fishing line. Repeated flexing and stretching of the knot will weaken it, and eventually, after hundreds of pulls, the knot may fail. It only takes a few seconds to re-tie, which is cheap insurance against knot failure. With just a little practice the improved clinch knot is among the simplest to tie and can be tied even at night without the aid of a flashlight.

PALOMAR KNOT

The Palomar knot is easy and quick to tie and it tests out nearly the same as the improved clinch but is far better when used with heavier lines. The Palomar can handle 60- to 100-pound test saltwater leaders with no problem.

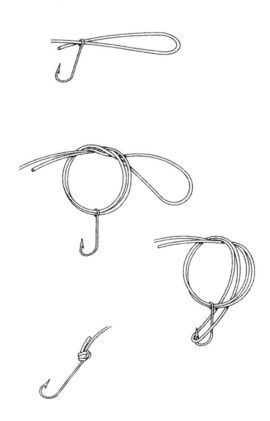

   The Palomar knot is very reliable and rarely slips once drawn up properly and drawn into place on the snap or swivel. Its criss-crossing coils spread the strain of the pull against the line over several stress points. Like the improved clinch knot, the Palomar should be re-tied after each day's fishing or after each big fish.

UNI-KNOT

The uni-knot is slightly more complicated to tie than the improved clinch or the Palomar, but it is an excellent knot to use when attaching terminal tackle. A major advantage is the knot's consistently high strength of up to 99 percent of the breaking strength of the unknotted line. A poorly tied uni-knot will usually test out better than a poorly tied clinch or Palomar.

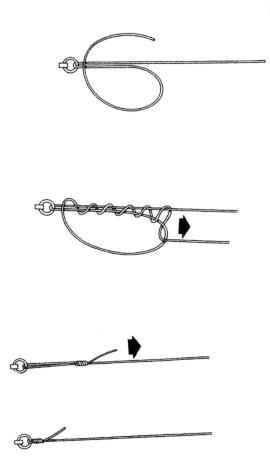

The knot gains exceptional strength because it adds an extra layer of the main fishing line beneath the knot coils. This effectively cushions the cutting forces as the knot is flexed and tensioned when casting or fighting a fish. The knot is durable and does not have to be re-tied after each fish or each day's fishing, although better fishermen will always re-tie as a matter of habit, just to be sure.

As you follow the directions and get to step three you'll find that the knot's coils come snug as the line is drawn up before the coils slide down the line to jam against the eye of the lure or snap. Be sure to wet the line so it is properly lubricated and to be sure the tightened coils don't fray the main line as the coils are drawn down.

SPIDER HITCH

Whenever two mono lines of unequal diameter are joined together, it's a good idea to use a Spider hitch or Bimini twist to double the lighter of the two lines. The knot of choice for adding leader is the surgeon's knot, which we'll cover in a few more pages. It gets high ratings for being easy to tie but it isn't known as a strong knot since it only tests at 85 percent of the breaking strength of the line. Adding a leader with the surgeon's knot directly to the main line will substantially weaken the main line by up to 25 percent. Because of the inherent weakness of the surgeon's knot, 30-pound test will be reduced to 24-pound test, 20-pound becomes 15-pound and 12-pound is reduced to 9-pound test.

The double line doubles the strength of the main fishing line so when the leader is added with the surgeon's knot the leader-to-double line connection is still far stronger than the main fishing line itself. Twenty-pound test line becomes 40-pound test at the double line. Any reduction in line strength at the surgeon's knot is far stronger than the unknotted main fishing line.

If the surgeon's knot is so weak, why use it? Alternative knots, like the Albright, are rather difficult and time consuming to tie. They test at 95 percent of the breaking strength of the line which is better than the surgeon's but that's still a reduction in the strength of the main fishing line. Once the double line is tied, the surgeon's knot is so much easier to tie; it wins as the knot of choice.

Of the two knots used to tie a double line, the spider hitch is far easier to tie and is especially well suited to lighter tackle of 6- to 30-pound test. Beyond 30-pound line, the knot gets difficult to tie and below 6-pound test it doesn't seem to hold its strength.

The spider hitch will test at 98 to 100 percent of the main fishing line so little or no line strength is lost in the transition from single to double line. Like all knots it should be wetted with saliva when drawn tight. Draw the coils down slowly and be sure they are even before snugging the coils tight. When first learning the spider hitch there is a tendency for the coils to wrap back over themselves so watch for this. If the coils don't look like the accompanying diagram, try the knot again.

The spider can break under sharp impact, and from repeated flexing. The older it gets, the weaker it gets. It's a good idea to get into the habit of re-tying terminal connections and leaders after each fishing trip anyhow so the spider will rarely fail you if you always tie fresh knots.

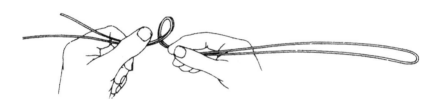

1. Form a double line loop of 24 to 36 inches. Near the tag end, twist the strands into a small reverse loop.

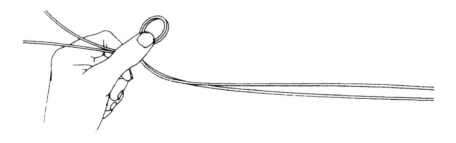

2. Hold the small loop between your left thumb and forefinger, with the thumb extended well above the finger.

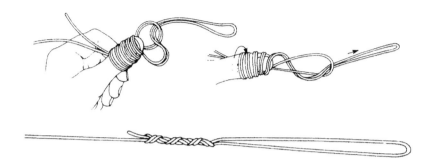

3. Wrap the double line strands around your thumb and the loop strands, making five parallel turns, and pass the end of the original big loop through the small loop. As you pull the loop, the five turns will pull off of the thumb. Be sure to pull the standing side and the tag end side of the loop equally. When the knot is seated, clip off the tag end.

BIMINI TWIST

Also called the 20 times around knot, the Bimini twist was first used by big game fishermen who needed to add strength to the end of their Dacron lines. A doubled section of line at the end of the line would be twice as strong as the main fishing line. Today's fishermen use the Bimini for light tackle, trolling, casting and big-game fishing, and it has become one of those universal knots that all salt-water anglers find useful.

Anyone who uses the Bimini regularly will agree that while this knot is not the easiest to tie, it is not the hardest either. Properly tied, with neat rolls and twists, it tests at 100 percent of the breaking strength of the main fishing line making the Bimini the best knot to use when a double line is needed. It is ideal for use with Dacron or mono lines of 10-pound test or stronger, but it is not well suited for super braid because of this line's slippery qualities.

Don't let the illustrations fool you. The Bimini only looks tricky. Tie it four or five times and you'll quickly get the hang of it.

1. Measure off a little more than twice the length of double line desired and double back forming the loop. For inshore trolling purposes the double line need only be about 2 to 4 feet in length.

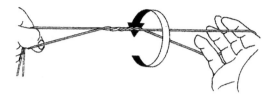

If you are right handed, grasp the standing line and tag end in your left hand, and insert the index and forefinger of your right hand inside the loop. Twist the two strands 20 times.

2. Keeping constant pressure on both ends of the loop, slip the open end over your knee. Hold the standing line in your left hand, the tag end in your right, and begin to spread your hands apart. This forces the coils to travel down the loop toward your knee.

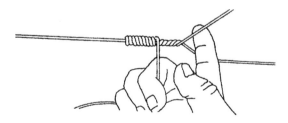

3. Bring your left hand to nearly vertical, and lower your right hand to a right angle to the twist. Insert the finger of the right hand into the loop and draw it toward the twists, while allowing the line grasped under tension in the right hand to slowly release line. I prefer to place the loop to a coffee cup hook works well at my workbench, but a reel handle will work well if you have to tie the

Bimini while at sea. Allow the forefinger of the right hand to "walk" the twists toward you. They will begin to roll over another. Gradually relax the tension on the tag end so it will roll over the column of twists.

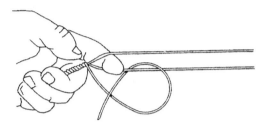

4. When the spiral of the tag end line has completely rolled over the column of twists, maintain your forefinger pressure on the loop, release the standing line and place a finger of that hand in the V or "crotch" where the loop "legs" project from the knot to prevent slippage of the last turn. Take a half-hitch with the tag end around the nearest "leg" of the loop and pull it tight.

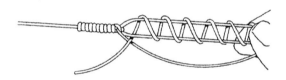

5. With the half-hitch holding the knot, relax the forefinger pressure but keep the loop stretched taut. Make five turns of the tag end around both loop legs, winding inside the bend of line formed by the loose half-hitch and toward the main knot.

6. Pull the tag end slowly, forcing the loops to gather in a tight spiral wrap. This prevents the Bimini from ever unraveling.

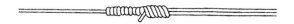

7. This is what a perfect Bimini twist should look like.

SURGEON'S KNOT

This is the handiest knot to use when joining two lines of significantly different diameters. It is easy to learn, easy to tie and convenient for adding heavy leaders for trolling. When connecting a super braid to a monofilament or fluorocarbon leader, double over the super line, and make a total of five turns through the loop.

1. Lay the line and leader parallel with an overlap of about eight inches.

2. Treat the two lines as a single line and tie an overhand knot, passing the entire leader through the loop. Leave the loop open.

3. Make a second overhand knot, again passing the whole leader and overlapped line through.

4. Hold both overlaps and pull in opposite directions to make the knot. Then pull the line only against the leader to set the knot. Clip the surplus ends close to the knot.

ALBRIGHT KNOT

Here's the strongest knot when adding a heavy leader to relatively light line, or to join a mono or fluorocarbon leader to a haywire loop formed at the end of a wire line. It's more difficult to tie than the surgeon's knot, but can be mastered in a few tries.

1. Double back a few inches of the heavy line (or wire) and pass about ten inches of the lighter line through the loop.

2. Wrap the light line back over itself and both strands of the heavy line. This is a bit easier if you hold the light line and both leader strands with your left thumb and forefinger, and wind with your right hand.

3. Make ten snug, neat wraps then pass the end of the line back through the original big loop, as shown.

4. While holding the coils in place, pull gently on both strands of the heavy line, causing the coils to move toward the end of the loop. Take out the slack by pulling on both strands of light line. When the knot is snug pull hard on the main light line and main heavy line. Pull as hard as you can for a good solid knot. Clip both excess tag ends close.

HAYWIRE TWIST

The haywire twist is the essential knot for making loops in single-strand wire line. The haywire may cause some slight loss of strength in the wire line if poorly tied. I've tested the haywire with a Hunter Spring Scale and have found that 40-pound test Malin stainless steel wire always broke above the 40-pound rating, but it broke every time at the knot. My nonscientific, workbench tests seem to show the haywire is very close to the strength of the unknotted wire line.

The informal tests did show a definite loss of strength when the knot was incorrectly tied. Using less than three twists of the wire caused the haywire to slip under extreme pressure as might happen when battling a big striped bass. Less than three wrapping or locking coils also caused the knot to slip and break. To be on the safe side always use at least five twists and five wrap coils when tying this knot to be sure of maximum strength.

There is a trick to tying the haywire that once learned makes tying this knot very easy. After making the loop and while holding the loop end between the fingers of the right hand, begin making the twists by gently pushing both hands towards each other. Each time the hands are rotated 180 degrees, a half twist is bent to the wire. The pushing motion helps the knot fold each twist neatly intertwined with one another. Ten rotations will put five complete twists into the wire.

The tightly spaced locking coils are much easier to make but it is important to make a smooth transition from the last twist into the first coil. Too abrupt a bend into the coil may cause the last twist to deform with a loss of knot strength.

Never cut the tag end of the wire line with pliers. The pliers will leave a razor-sharp edge at the end of the wire that can cause severe cuts. Bending a crank handle into the tag end allows the wire to be easily broken so it breaks cleanly with no protruding sharp edge to slice a finger.

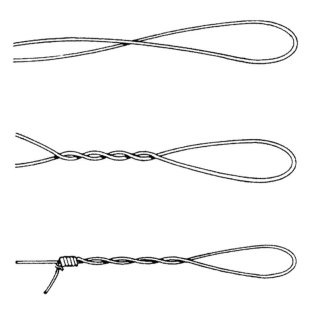

1. Pass several inches of the tag end of the wire through the hook eye. Bend the tag back next to the standing wire to form a small loop.

2. Hold the loop firmly with the thumb and forefinger of your left hand. Form a wide V between the two wire strands. Both sections of wire must be twisted simultaneously, or else the tag will simply wrap around the standing wire, producing a much weaker connection.

3. Make at least five twists (ten half turns) in the two legs of the wire. Next, bend the tag end so it is 90 degrees to the standing wire.

4. Hold the already twisted section and wrap the tag end around the standing wire in several neat, tight, parallel coils.

5. Bend the last inch or so of the tag to a right angle, bending away from the standing line, not over it, to form a "handle."

6. Hold the twist steady and rock the tag end back and forth. It should break quickly, leaving a smooth end at the twist. If the wire is cut at this stage of the twist, it will leave a sharp burr that can cut your hand.

The haywire twist is any easy knot to tie after only a little practice. If your first few don't turn out so hot, have patience and try a few more. Once you get the knack of it, you'll never lose the technique. It's like riding a bicycle; you just never forget how to do it.

LOOP-TO-LOOP CONNECTIONS

Two loops can be linked together when rigging a wire-line outfit to form a very strong connection between Dacron backing and wire, and between the wire and the mono leader. The loop-to-loop connection system requires that a loop be tied into the end of the wire line with a haywire twist, and into the Dacron backing with a Spider hitch or a Bimini twist, and into the mono leader with a surgeon's loop, Spider hitch or Bimini twist.

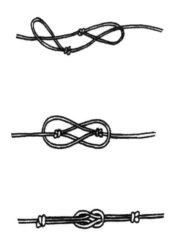

When connecting the wire to the Dacron backing, make a haywire twist in the tag end of the wire line while it is still wound on the packaging spool, and make a Spider or Bimini in the backing.

After both loops are made, pass the backing loop through the hay-wire and continue to pull the backing loop until the spool of wire can be passed completely through it. Pass the backing around the wire spool a second time. Slowly pull the lines until the loops seat snugly as shown in the illustration.

To add a mono leader, pass the haywire loop through the loop in the mono, then pull the mono tag end through the haywire. Pull both lines until the loops seat properly.

About the Author

Pete Barrett has been writing about his fishing experiences along the East Coast for the past 40 years and has published over 1200 feature stories. His travels have taken him from New England to the Outer Banks of North Carolina, Florida and the Bahamas, and he operated the charter boat "Linda B" for over 25 years for inshore and offshore fishing from the Manasquan River in New Jersey. Pete recently retired after 35 years with The Fisherman magazine, but continues to write about his fishing adventures and is a frequent speaker at seminars and shows.

A strong advocate of tag and release fishing, he has won several national and regional awards for his tagging efforts, and he is a firm believer in conserving and protecting gamefish from commercial overfishing and overly restrictive, unscientific regulations promoted by extreme environmentalists. Pete is a representative of the International Game Fish Association and a member of the Recreational Fishing Alliance advisory board, and has served on several state and federal gamefish management organizations, including the International Commission for the Conservation of Atlantic Tuna and the original committee that developed the Striped Bass Management Plan.

Pete and his wife, Linda, fish spring, summer and fall for striped bass, bluefish, fluke and weakfish; and for snook, trout and southern species in the winter. Their son, Rich, is a full-time captain fishing from New England through Florida, Bermuda, Mexico and the Bahamas.

Index